Advance praise for
WHO DOES HE SAY YOU ARE?

"In *Who Does He Say You Are?*, Colleen Mitchell delves deep into the
mystery of God's abundant mercy that transforms our hearts and draws
us near to him. With gripping stories, guided prayer, and reflection
questions at the end of each chapter, you will put this book down
encouraged and excited to be who you were created to be
—a woman in the image and likeness of God!"
—KELLY WAHLQUIST, author, *Created to Relate*
and founder of W.I.N.E. (Women in the New Evangelization)

"This book is a heart-stirring anthem for women who need a fresh
reminder of their truest identity. Colleen Mitchell writes with refreshing
clarity and depth, bringing the stories of biblical women into clear
focus for us today, no matter our circumstances.
I highly recommend this beautifully written book."
—JENNIFER DUKES LEE, author, *The Happiness Dare* and *Love Idol*

"Colleen Mitchell's voice is that of an understanding, honest friend.
Her reflections, solidly grounded in Scripture, introduce us to women
whose journeys lead them to new life in Christ in unexpected ways,
assuring us that with an open, hopeful heart, their destination might be
ours as well. *Who Does He Say You Are?* is an excellent resource
for individuals and small groups seeking substantive,
engaging study and discussion materials."
—AMY WELBORN, author, *Wish You Were Here: Travels through Loss
and Hope* and *A Catholic Woman's Book of Days*

"This beautifully written book drew me into the hearts of biblical
women, and there, I understood anew Christ's great love for them. As
I lingered, I grew to know what that love means for me. This volume
has biblical depth and maturity without being out of reach. Skillfully
textured, it is rich and real and truly worthy of our time and attention.
I will be forever grateful for the gift of this book's important message."
—ELIZABETH FOSS, wife and mother to nine, Catholic blogger, and
coauthor, *Small Steps for Catholic Moms*

"Colleen Mitchell is a woman who knows the Lord—through his Word, through the sacraments, through deep and fervent prayer. *Who Does He Say You Are?* comes from a deep place of searching for answers and finding her identity in Christ. This beautiful book is part memoir, part guidebook, part invitation to the personal transformation that is possible when we draw near to the Lord and allow him to walk beside us through our sometimes messy lives. Let Colleen introduce you in a fresh way to women of the Gospels whose lives were changed by Jesus. Sit with her and meditate on their stories— and allow your own heart to be transformed."
—SARAH CHRISTMYER, coauthor, *The Great Adventure* Catholic Bible Study Program

"When tragedy comes for us, we only want to go back and be who we were before it struck—the mother of the living child, the wife of the faithful husband, the healthy woman who thought she could, just maybe, do it all. But when there's no going back, each of us faces another important question: If I'm not that woman anymore, then who am I? Mitchell's wise, impassioned portraits of our mothers and sisters in the faith helps us to answer that difficult question for ourselves."
—JESSICA MESMAN GRIFFITH, Christopher Award–winning author, *Love and Salt* and cocreator, "Sick Pilgrim"

WHO DOES HE SAY YOU ARE?

[WOMEN TRANSFORMED BY
CHRIST IN SCRIPTURE]

servant
AN IMPRINT OF
FRANCISCAN MEDIA
Cincinnati, Ohio

Scripture passages have been taken from *New Revised Standard Version Bible*, copyright ©1989 by the Division of Christian Education of the National Council of the Churches of Christ in the U.S.A., and used by permission. All rights reserved.

Cover design by Mary Ann Smith
Book design by Mark Sullivan

LIBRARY OF CONGRESS CATALOGING-IN-PUBLICATION DATA
Names: Mitchell, Colleen (Catholic Missionary), author.
Title: Who does he say that you are? : women transformed by Christ in scripture / Colleen Mitchell.
Description: Cincinnati : Servant, 2016.
Identifiers: LCCN 2016015577 | ISBN 9781632531025 (trade paper)
Subjects: LCSH: Women in the Bible. | Bible. New Testament—Criticism, interpretation, etc. | Women—Religious aspects—Christianity. | Catholic women—Religious life.
Classification: LCC BS2445 .M55 2016 | DDC 226/.092082—dc23
LC record available at https://lccn.loc.gov/2016015577

ISBN 978-1-63253-102-5

Published by Servant
an imprint of Franciscan Media
28 W. Liberty St.
Cincinnati, OH 45202
www.FranciscanMedia.org

Printed in the United States of America.
Printed on acid-free paper.
17 18 19 20 5 4 3 2

• • • • •

To all the women I call
mother, sister, family, or friend,
and to the ones I hope to one day call
daughter—this is for you.
Embrace who you are in him.

• • • • •

CONTENTS

· · · · ·

· · · · ·

The origins of this book were first scratched onto the back pages of a prayer journal as I sat in patches of wild forget-me-nots on the banks of a river in rural Costa Rica. I was living some of the most beautiful—and the most difficult—moments of my life.

My husband, children, and I had headed to that spot in Costa Rica as a mission field after three years of being immersed in deep, dark pain. In 2009, our seemingly healthy infant son inexplicably stopped breathing; we buried him in a wooden casket too tiny to contain my devastation.

Five months later, I was pregnant again, barely able to consider the hope of another life growing inside me, yet clinging to its promise. Then, while lying on a table in my doctor's office, I saw a tiny body floating motionless in the darkness of my womb, and I was unable to bear the all-too-final verdict of "No heartbeat." A year later, again a little one dreamed of and hoped for was gone before he was ever ours to hold.

My heartbreaking sorrow consumed me, yet I tried with all my might to find a way back to who I had been before, to be mother and wife and sister and friend again. In addition to the pain of losing our children, my husband lost a dream job that burst into our lives like a miracle and fizzled out like a wet match. Finances stretched to the breaking point. Relationships with friends and within our faith community strained under the weight of our sorrow. Our hearts strained too. And that place where two are hearts are made one? Well, it ached with the burden as well. I felt as though the sinews of love that once held us together in one seamless entity now had a tenuous grasp.

With each wave of grief and worry, the fractured pieces of my heart floated further and further away from me, and I could not conceive of how to pull myself back together again.

Everywhere I looked in my life, I saw sorrow. Yet, even as I felt myself breaking open, I clung to the assurance that God was in this. I looked for the intimate signs of his presence in our lives, and I begged him to redeem our suffering. I called these signs "tender mercies"—the ways I could count that God was there, in the details of my days, reminding me that he had me and that I was still his, such as a nighttime phone call from a friend just as the anxiety and fear threatened to overwhelm me, a conversation with a priest who had just the right words to console me, and the quiet reminders in nature that God was still God and he was still good.

I leaned on the rhythm of the sacred liturgy of the Catholic Church to carry me over the waves of emotions that I experienced. I thanked God for the ancient words of the Mass and the traditions of my Catholic faith that walked me through my grief. I felt supported by the wisdom of two thousand years of human experience and grateful for the way the Church can be Christ present for the sorrowing and the suffering. Our child's godfather, a priest, spent hours at our home offering wise counsel, loyal friendship, and the grace of the sacraments. I didn't see it then, but in all those moments a secret healing was beginning inside me, readying me to draw near to God once again and be transformed by him. I knew my faith, and its practices were consoling me in ways nothing else could, but in time I would see that there was more happening than that—that a deposit of grace was building in my soul, even in the midst of my sorrow, which would, in due season, roll the stone away from my heart and release rays of resurrection joy.

We were broken and holding on to that faith like a life raft when God shone his light onto a little corner of the earth, made a crooked path straight, and said, "Go." Shortly after our son Bryce's death, my husband felt the Spirit's leading to form a nonprofit organization in Bryce's name for the purpose of sharing the Gospel. I can't say I opposed the idea, but I could not make logical sense of how you give your heart away when you are holding its shards in bleeding hands. But I was begging God to redeem our pain, and I wasn't going to deny my husband an opportunity to lead us to that healing; so I finally consented and stoically stayed mostly out of his way. St. Bryce Missions was born in the spring of 2010. As all around me I saw new life blooming, a tiny seed of healing took root in my heart. In time this seed, tilled by my faith and watered with God's hope, would blossom within the soil of my heart into new life for me too—but I was still too raw in my pain to see it.

A few months later, as fall's breezes began to blow through, my husband came home from spending nearly three weeks working on a business project in Costa Rica, recounting tales of high mountains and a group of little-known indigenous people in need of hearing the Gospel message. I could hear in the trailing of his voice that he had already surrendered a part of his heart to that place. And I could feel behind the heavy beating of my own heart that God was pushing me, giving me a direction.

I had prayed for redemption and deliverance, yet Costa Rica seemed like a faraway place to me, a fantasy land, a place where I'd be able to speak my son's name without shattering into a million pieces. I dug in my heels and railed at God. I put up a wall of anger and refused to budge. I was angry that redemption looked more like me serving God and others than him coming to my rescue. And mostly, I was terrified to let go of the place I was in. The pain had become comfortable. I had shined up our lives with a glossy veneer of happiness, running from activity to activity, overcommitting myself, and steering clear of vulnerability. I was addicted to my own competency and perceived strength in the same way a person becomes addicted to prescription painkillers.

And even as I rehearsed the articulate arguments in my head and rallied my passions to fight, I knew God was doing this new thing, and I was going to have to give in eventually. But I didn't go down without a fight. I wanted to believe that there was a way out of my pain, but my heart ached to know that the way through would be the way back. I wished with all my heart that there was a way to go back to the woman I had been and the life I had before my Bryce's death. Moving forward to a profoundly different life was scary because it meant accepting that there was no going back. Redemption meant acknowledging my scars and my pain and letting resurrection hope come in the form God was offering it, rather than the way I was trying to force it. I sat with the Word of God in quiet moments and looked for his instructions. I looked long on my favorite image of his Mother, her baby in one hand and a small lamb in the other, and asked her to show me how to walk through this life she knew so well. I found saints who would become faithful guides as I wrestled toward surrender.

That surrender came one morning when the tension that filled our home sent my husband off to Mass looking for his peace and me to my knees begging God for the strength to offer him my yes. I finally offered myself to him as I was—afraid and unable to see how I could be of use to him—and prayed that if he still wanted me, I would go. When I finally made that surrender to God and to the vision my husband was now seeing for our future with certain clarity, God moved mountains to show me that he was arranging this for me. And so, a few short months later, I packed up my five boys, my memories, and my weak-kneed yes, along with all the necessities of life into twelve suitcases, and embarked sight unseen on a journey of redemption in the Chirripo Mountains of south central Costa Rica: home of the Cabecar indigenous peoples, clear rivers, and patches of wild forget-me-nots. And there, I found freedom and healing.

Even though we had come to this place to be missionaries, to reach out to others, the first eight weeks were like rehab for my soul. God tore me away from all the noise I was using to drown out my pain and began to fill the chasms with his Word and his presence instead. We committed ourselves to spend one hour a day as a family adoring Christ in the Eucharist in the little chapel in our new home. I woke every morning and spent time reading his Word on our front porch as the jungle came to life around me. Then I walked the dirt road that led to that little chapel and sat in stillness and silence while he spoke to me. I journaled pages and pages of thoughts and prayers and, yes, even thanksgiving. I began to remember God's vision for who I am, to hear him remind me of who it was he made me to be, by drawing near to him in prayer and reading the Scriptures, which had always been my favorite way to encounter Jesus and build my relationship with him. In that prayer, I began to own that even with all the cracks and broken places the last few years had wrought in me, I was beautiful and beloved to him, and I had a purpose. He wanted to use me. I found myself lonely and quiet and treasured by my God on my tiny front porch in a tucked-away place called *Grano de Oro*, or "grain of gold." It was winter in the States, and an unexpected chill was blowing our way, but here in my new life, the sun was shining and my heart was beginning to warm in its glow.

Our lives took another painful turn a few weeks later when we received the news that my mother-in-law, precious Granny to my five boys, was dying. Cancer was taking her away faster than we were prepared to let her go. In the rush of decision-making and emergency flight booking, I didn't pause to think much about what this process was going to do to our newly mended hearts. I just knew I had to get my husband to his mother. I sent him off with our oldest son and suddenly found myself alone with four boys in a remote place where I could barely communicate. We were grieving once again, and this time with no escape hatch.

The riverbank in our little town, just behind our house, became our coping place. As soon as the sun was high enough in the sky to warm its waters each day, we crept through the coffee grove, pulled back the barbed-wire fence that held in the cows and the pigs, and made our way to the river's healing waters. I spread out a towel and sat, Bible in lap, and begged God to keep putting me back together even as these new cracks formed in my heart, while little boys focused on building dams out of rocks and rode banana-tree logs down the currents. We breathed in the fresh air of the mountains and counted fireflies as dusk whispered in the tall grass. And somehow, we found our way through the grief, and I found my way back to intimate friendship with Christ, back to who he says that I really am.

There, in that place where my pain and my healing collided, God met me—in his Word, in his Eucharistic presence, in the quiet stillness of my new life. In the person of Jesus, he showed me his love, his desires for me, his healing touch, and his intimate knowledge of both my suffering and my hopes. He drew near to me and beckoned me to draw near to him. In the stories of the women of the Gospels, he showed me myself and he reminded me of who he was. And then he said, "And this is who I say that you are."

I tucked the message away in my heart like a secret between two lovers. I learned life and grief and growth in my new place. But a year later, the stories were still there, beating inside me like a drum that needed to be heard. I scribbled them out once again in the back of yet another journal, and I consented to write them if God was asking me to.

Soon after, life went from lonely and quiet to the wild ride of a blossoming full-time ministry and the work of growing a nonprofit from the ground up while still mothering my five sons and building a marriage. Life was full, and I found my stride in its rhythm. I started to feel whole again—and purposeful. And it was good.

But with time, the stories and the message of God's heart that healed my broken places swelled inside me until they were full and ready to break forth. They began to push against my insides, insisting on being born, whether I could figure out how to make time for it or not. And somehow the time was there, and the words came.

The God of the heavens and the earth wants you too to remember who it is that he says that you are. Very likely, I do not know your story. Yours may read a lot like mine, or it may be altogether different. But I do know this: wherever you are in that story, God desires to draw near to you and remind you who you are. In the midst of your cracks and suffering and hard places and pain, he has a love letter to offer you. He handed it to your sisters of the Gospels in person. He hands it to you now through their stories. And I believe that in these stories there is healing and grace and purpose for you. There is wholeness and newness for the having.

And I know with every fiber of my being that God wants that for you. Because he says that you are loved by him.

~ BEFORE YOU BEGIN ~

I hope you will find between these pages a mirror that reflects back to you the image of God in which you were created. And I hope that, in that image, you will be reminded of the woman you are meant to be. Whether you come to these pages in the midst of a darkness or pain you cannot bear, or with the anticipation and joy of a new dream in your hands or a newly healed place in your heart, I pray that he will meet you here, in the stories of your sisters, and build a vision for your life and your future that is whole and lovely and with a unique purpose. Whether you know God well and have walked with him long or you are a new friend to Christ who is just learning his ways and how to walk with him, I believe you will find something in these pages that will draw you deeper into the heart of your Savior.

Even before we fully enter into the Gospel story, in the Gospel of Matthew, we find an invitation to women to see themselves as part of this story. As Matthew recounts the genealogy of Jesus (Matthew 1:1–17), we find included a list of Old Testament women, mothers of sons and wives of husbands, traced through the history of salvation. The women included in that list were faithful, heroic participants in the kingdom story that played itself out before the coming of the Christ, the Messiah. None of them was perfect. Each had her own tale of difficulty and sorrow to bear. But each also was blessed for her faithfulness by God's drawing near to her and fulfilling his promises. We might wonder why Matthew would include those women in such a genealogy. I think the answer may be twofold.

First, because the Scriptures are the inspired Word of God, we can trust that it was his idea that those women's names showed up in the line of Jesus's ancestry. Perhaps he wanted to impress upon us that women have always been a part of the salvation story, that we have always been in his heart, that we have always had a place in the reality of redemption. Tamar, Ruth, Bathsheba, and Rahab—we look back at them as hints of what was to come, glimpses of the role women were to play in the story of the Messiah. The feminine heart held the messianic hope in a special way from the earliest of days, and saw that hope fulfilled when Christ finally came. Our sisters knew what it was to have their stories and their hearts transformed by drawing near to God in the divine person of Christ.

The second part of our answer lies in the story of the last woman mentioned in Matthew's genealogy, "Mary, of whom Jesus was born, who is called the Messiah" (Matthew 1:16). In Mary, womanhood reaches it perfection and its peak. Women of faith in the Old Testament reached for her from one side of history, while we her daughters who ponder the Gospels reach for her from the other side. She is the anchor of our hope for all that we as women might be, the true reflection of a heart perfectly transformed by Christ, fully redeemed. And she is our model of what it means to bring the hope of Christ out into our world once we have come to know who we are in him. Mary completes the waiting hope of the women of the Old Testament, and she guides us on our own path as we find, not only who we are in Jesus, but all the possibilities of who we can be if we allow him to draw near to us and transform us with grace and mercy.

Mary remains an ever-present figure as we journey through the Gospels with the women who meet Jesus. These stories are the tales of very different women, yet the common thread is the one most powerfully illustrated by his own Mother: intimacy with Jesus calls out the very best of who we can be as women. To the extent that we allow him to make us who he knows we are, we will be able to walk in the story he desires to write with our lives.

For this reason, you will find mention of Mary woven through the stories of the women we meet in this book. In some stories, she plays a prominent part, as it is written in the Gospels, and in others, she is more of a quiet presence. But always her presence is there as a hopeful reminder of what is possible for us. We are women created to reflect the glory of God and invited to know him and love him in unique intimacy. Mary is the height of that experience, and she is a loving guide in whose footsteps we can confidently follow. Look for her as you make your way through these stories, and consider how her presence and example might serve to guide you as you discover what it might mean to know who you are in Christ and build your identity on that reality.

~ How to Use This Book ~

In practical terms, each chapter of the book offers you the opportunity to dig into the Word of God and meet for the first time or see anew one of the women in the Gospels. And in her story, you can consider what God is saying to you about who he is and who he has made you to be. The Scripture citation is offered at the outset of the chapter, and I would encourage you to read it from your favorite version of the Bible before reading the chapter any further. You can read the verses there, but truly, the chapter is designed for you to visit the story repeatedly in your own Bible as you work through it. Your reflection will be richer for having reached into the pages of your own personal Bible and dug around a bit in these stories, looking for what came just before and after, seeing the words laid out on the page for yourself. This book uses the *New Revised Standard Version: Catholic Edition* of the Bible, but you will find the same insight into the stories in whatever translation you use. The book is your guide, but your Bible is your real teacher. Sit with them both together, and be transformed by what they have to show you.

In the pages that follow the Scripture citation, you will find the messages that the Lord used to mend me and give me new hope in the days beside the river. I hope you will hear him speak to you as well. I pray you will look for the ways he is reaching out to your heart and drawing near to you and your unique story in each reflection. These are the stories of my remaking, and I believe they can be yours as well.

After the reflection, you will find an invitation to apply the lesson we have learned from each woman's story to your own life and faith journey. This section offers you an opportunity to consider not only the woman's transformation in her encounter with Christ, but your own. It guides you to consider the invitation her story is extending to you to experience new depth in your relationship with Christ and closer unity with him.

Next you will find a prayer that you can use to respond to God and what he has offered you in his Word. At its heart, prayer is simply conversation with God. For some of us, that comes very naturally. For others, it is harder. We fumble hesitantly for the words and feel as if we are talking to the air. Wherever you fall on that spectrum, I encourage you really to pray these prayers rather than simply read them, to speak to God like the friend that he is, and to know that he sees beyond your words, whether they are laced with eloquence or plagued with awkwardness, to the longings of your heart. And I would encourage you to take that prayer and make it the beginning of a personal conversation with the Christ, the Messiah. Consider it not the end of the chapter but the beginning of a closer relationship, as you return to the Word regularly—letting him speak to you intimately and show you who you are in his eyes—and as you respond to his leading.

Lastly, at the end of each chapter, I have offered you some questions for further reflection about where you are and where God might want to bring you along this journey of encouragement through the Gospels. These questions can be adapted easily for a group study of the book, for private journaling, or simply for quiet reflection. I do encourage you to spend the time in prayer to formulate the answers to at least some of these questions. I think we can often surprise ourselves with our answers and see something we never expected to see in our responses. However you choose to use them, I do hope they will be a guide to processing what God is doing in you as he calls you to a deeper intimacy with him through the stories of the women of the Gospels.

In the end, everything in the chapter—everything in these pages—is meant to be a tool to help you draw nearer to the God who created you, who loves you, and who wants to see you whole, knowing who you are in him and purposeful in your pursuit of the life that leads you to him. If you ask him to use these words according to his purpose, I know he will respond faithfully. If you ask him to show you in the stories of your biblical sisters who it is that he says you are, I know you will be encouraged.

Thank you for walking this journey with me and giving me the chance to share with you the Good News that breathed life into my soul. This journey truly brought healing to my heart and gave me direction in my faith walk and confidence in my relationship with God once again. I hope you find the same in these pages, and know that I carry each of you in my heart.

Read on. He has been waiting anxiously to draw near and remind you of who you are.

------ ∞ ------

CHAPTER ONE

"You Are a Dwelling Place of the Most High God"

Mary, the Mother of Jesus

In the sixth month the angel Gabriel was sent by God to a town in Galilee called Nazareth, to a virgin engaged to a man whose name was Joseph, of the house of David. The virgin's name was Mary. And he came to her and said, "Greetings, favored one! The Lord is with you." But she was much perplexed by his words and pondered what sort of greeting this might be. The angel said to her, "Do not be afraid, Mary, for you have found favor with God. And now, you will conceive in your womb and bear a son, and you will name him Jesus. He will be great, and will be called the Son of the Most High...and of his kingdom there will be no end."

Mary said to the angel, "How can this be, since I am a virgin?" The angel said to her, "The Holy Spirit will come upon you, and the power of the Most High will overshadow you; therefore the child to be born will be holy; he will be called Son of God. And now, your relative Elizabeth in her old age has also conceived a son; and this is the sixth month for her who was said to be barren. For nothing will be impossible with God."

Then Mary said, "Here am I, the servant of the Lord; let it be with me according to your word." Then the angel departed from her.

—Luke 1:26–38

· · · · ·

When I was younger, it bothered me when Jesus addressed his Mother as "Woman" in the Gospels. This was long before I had grown into my own womanhood, or knew what it meant to be a woman. Now I hear that word in a new light.

"Woman," he calls her. Archetypal, she is not just one woman among many, but the Woman, just as Eve was "woman" at creation. In her very being, Mary embodies all of womanhood's beauty, goodness, and grace. She is as woman was created to be. She first embarked on the journey of walking with the Savior so the rest of us might follow. She shows us what it means to live as a woman overshadowed by the Spirit. And the first thing she teaches us about womanhood is the only thing we really need to know: *God dwells in us.*

God could have chosen to break upon the scene of human history to save us from our very selves in any way he wanted. It could have been in a way that was overtly grand and glorious and terrifying. He could have shaken the foundations of the earth with his coming and darkened the universe only to light it up again. He could have put on a fantastic show.

But he chose instead to create a vessel that could cradle his greatness—he chose to be borne by and born of a woman. The glory that happens in the womb of a woman may just be God's best show of all. And the idea that our salvation is both borne and born in a world that scarcely knows it has a reason to hope? That God is working out the salvation of the world in secret ways with a woman as his only companion? What deep, rich grace there is in that!

God's secret workings inside one woman are the beginning of human salvation. I can hardly bear the beauty of that sometimes—especially when I am reminded how often I am inattentive to the ways God is working in me, or even wholly rebellious to them. But in Mary, I am reminded that when the beautiful mystery of womanhood intertwines with the great mystery of God, the miracle of salvation can be born. In Mary, I have a picture of womanhood at its height, an untainted vessel full of grace carrying the light of Christ out into the world. I want to live pregnant with that hope: that God dwelling in me can unfold into a grace and salvation that pours out to others. I want to be ever attentive to the mystery of God active in me, as Mary was the moment she heard the angel's greeting sound in her ears.

When we look at Mary here at the moment of the annunciation, when our Creator God tucked himself inside her virgin womb, we learn something about our own womanhood. In what is happening in that one woman's body and soul to bring about the salvation of the world, we learn a powerful truth about ourselves: God designed us to house his glory.

He meant to dwell in us. The design of our bodies reflects the design of our souls: receptive, nurturing, life-giving. God designed as a first earthly home for himself the perfect vessel, the receptacle of grace without flaw, and it was a woman, Mary. And so Mary shows us what it means to be woman, to have a feminine soul that is meant to receive life-giving love, to gestate that life with expectant hope, and to bear it out into the world through the hard work that it is to labor. This is our spiritual calling as much as it is our physical being. This calling is not dependent on whether or not you ever bear a babe in your womb; it is yours because you bear the babe called King of kings inside you.

He dwells in you—redeeming, loving, saving from right there in the very center of your being. You, sister, can live full of grace too. There may not be angel's wings and glory rays to announce his presence. But do not doubt that he longs to live in you, to be made incarnate in you. He wants to dwell within you so that your very flesh magnifies him out into the world.

"How can this be?" Mary asks, and we echo the question with her. How does this happen, that the God of the universe comes to dwell inside us? It happens to us, friend, just as the angel told Mary it would. He overshadows us. Sometimes it feels as if we spend our whole lives just trying to step out of the shadows, doesn't it? To be noticed. To get out of the darkness someone else has cast over us. To find the light.

But the answer to our ultimate joy is found under his shadow. One synonym for the word *overshadow* is "hover." God hovers over Mary so that he can dwell within her. He overshadows her. And she lets him. She agrees to let him shine while she hides in his shadow. She offers herself as a lowly servant, a slave even, to the overshadowing presence of God dwelling within her.

I have offered God my fair share of uncertain yeses in my life, and I have seen what he can do with just a little bit of faith surrendered to his will. I wonder what more he might do with me if I could offer the kind of yes Mary does—so fully surrendered to his desires for her, so willing to let him draw near to her, that she calls herself his servant girl, his slave, and allows him to overshadow her own will and desires with those he has for her. She gives herself completely to the identity God is creating for her and in her, rather than struggling to hold on to her own expectations and plans.

I mean, Mary was engaged to be married to Joseph. She planned a simple life as the wife of a carpenter in her small town, likely just down the road from her parents. She prayed the prayers of a faithful Jewish girl and lived the life of one too. To suddenly be asked to take on a completely new identity meant she would need to give all of herself over to God, the deepest parts of her, where all her hopes and dreams and fears and longing lay, and to trust that his presence dwelling in her would overshadow all of that with light and grace.

This is our key to being a Christ-bearer: to allow Christ to enter the deepest parts of us so that we might bear the presence of he who is called Most High in our very being. He asks to dwell in us. And when we offer our "yes," when we offer ourselves fully to serve his purposes, he comes to dwell in us. He draws near and places his shadow over us, his presence growing within us while his Spirit surrounds us. And we are transformed by that overshadowing. We are made more fully who we are by the intimate presence of Christ drawing so close to us that he sees us from the inside out.

Who could ever conceive that God could be conceived? That he could dwell with us? And yet, this is how he always meant for it to be. In the Genesis days, he strolled in the garden that was Adam and Eve's home. He walked in their midst. He dwelled among them. This is what it means to be saved, to be redeemed: he dwells with us, and we are his people. He dwells in you. God's greatest longing is to draw near to you and for you to receive him in love.

And when we say yes to his request to come close to us, he fills us with a new hope. When we agree to become God's dwelling place, he takes up residence in us. We swell inside with hope, with grace, with the message of salvation. His presence grows in us. He is magnified in us. We grow so full with him that we cannot contain his presence within ourselves anymore, and we labor with the burden of love. Life is born of his presence within us, and it begs for release. The sound of salvation echoes inside us until it can no longer be contained.

So we give ourselves over to it, and we allow it to be released into this wild, wide world, desperate for its cries of freedom. In Spanish, the phrase used for giving birth, for pushing life into the world, is *dar a luz*, "to give light." And isn't this so true of our calling? We allow the Light of the world to come and dwell in us; we receive him. He grows in the intimacy of our souls until we swell to bursting, and then we spend our lives "giving light," pushing the Light of life out into the world so that the world too may know him. Mary is the ultimate illumination of a woman filled with Christ's presence, of a woman lit up from within by grace. We can offer ourselves to God in full surrender with great confidence because we can see in Mary the beauty of a womanhood that blossoms to its own fullness by allowing God to fill her.

~ WHO DOES HE SAY YOU ARE? ~
AN INVITATION TO LET GOD DWELL IN YOU

Who doesn't love a good birth story? There is a sense of sisterhood tied in the tales of our labors and births. There are no two labor stories that are just the same, and not all women's stories have happy endings. Some of us grieve from having a story that seems not to be a story at all, from the birth wished for that never came, or from the desire expected but never present. And yet, still, we connect with the strength and beauty of womanhood revealed in our stories of birth, of giving light.

Is it not the same with our spiritual stories? Each is different. Some are simple and straightforward, others miraculously joyous, some still being lived and written, some miscarried before their time, some feeling the weight of ever trying and never bearing fruit. But these are our stories of birth, and in them we find our common connection.

We stand together under the shadow of the Spirit, and the

Most High God comes to dwell in us—in you and me. It only takes our yes. And the yes releases the wild grace of growth, of swelling hope in us, of an intimate relationship with the One who is saving us even as we carry him. And when we have grown full and stretched wide to cradle this light, we open ourselves to its pushing, and it spills out of us, a love and a light that brings saving life to all who long for it.

I have had times when the stretching and the pulling were unwelcomed, when I would have preferred to stay tightly wound in my own space, cradling in my womb my own plans and what I thought I needed from God. But the truth is, no hope is born of that closing in on ourselves. There is no great mystery burgeoning with new spiritual life for the world in my own human desires. Only God has that kind of hope and love to offer me, to offer the world. And he leans close and asks me to be a conduit that both contains and nurtures that saving love and then spills it out to a world in need of it.

Mary's is the ultimate birth story. She walked through her life at Jesus's side, loving him with a real human love and at the same time fully understanding his divine purpose. She bore the tension of living in perfect joy and complete sorrow as she watched her baby boy become our Redeemer. Her life with Christ was not always an easy one. She suffered alongside her Son. She pondered and she hoped and she loved, and she surrendered herself fully to the story of salvation and her part in it. Just as she gave herself fully to God in the annunciation, though she was not fully sure of what it all meant or how it would come to pass, Mary continues to offer herself as an example of what we can be if we too will open our hearts for him to draw near and dwell in us.

Can you feel it? That it is worth it—all it takes to get there on this journey? You don't have to understand it all or know how it will all happen before it does. You can just stand up and say, "Yes, let it be as you say in me," and then become a cradle of grace, a womb of love, where the Most High God dwells.

Oh, the wild glory and grace of it all! We are the women who follow in the footsteps of Woman. Mary is our first example of what it means to be a woman who has a relationship with Jesus. She is the first one to know him and to love him. And she is all the possibility of womanhood fully revealed to us. She is a vessel of hope and a cradle of love who nurtures a quiet intimacy with Jesus and then sacrifices herself to offer him to the world.

And this too is who we are, we women. All of us are made in the same model of her whom Jesus called "Woman." Mary was the woman who was both his creation and his Mother. We are her sisters and her daughters. And we too are dwelling places of the Most High God. By her example, we can live overshadowed by God, be his dwelling places, and bear Christ—he who is our salvation and light—both inside ourselves in intimate sacredness and out into the world in the laboring act of faith.

Have you given him permission to dwell in you? Are you ready to do so? It only requires your quiet yes. Can you feel me, whispering it with you, standing by your side under his shadow, pregnant with the hope of salvation? Let us labor together to offer this hope to the waiting world.

~ LET US PRAY ~

My Jesus, Savior of the World and God Most High, thank you for desiring to dwell in me. Thank you for having made me to receive you, to cradle your presence within me, to bear your life out into a world that needs you desperately.

I kneel in the radiance of your glory and wonder how it could possibly be that I am meant to bear that kind of hope within me. But you assure me that all you need is my simple yes, that you will do the rest. You assure me that all you ask is that I rest in the shadow of your love and let you hover over me.

You have made it so easy for me, Lord, to become a Christ-bearer. And yet, still too often, I waver in declaring my yes. I am distracted by the how and not willing to trust in your wisdom. I desire to offer my yes but find myself stalling.

Forgive me, Lord. Help me to remember the young girl who stood to lose everything and still gave herself to you, offered herself as maid, servant, dwelling place. She stood in your shadow and let you be magnified in her. O Lord, how I want to be that kind of woman, perfect in obedience and full of the highest of hopes. Send your Spirit, Lord, and bid him hover. Stay over me; cover me. In the shadow of your love, I can find the courage. I can say yes. I will be a cradle of grace, and I will sing with gladness. I will call you Christ, Messiah, Most High, and I will let you be magnified in my soul.

Love incarnate, my salvation, come.

Dwell in me, Lord. I am yours. Amen.

~ QUESTIONS FOR REFLECTION ~

1. What does it mean to me that God designed me as a woman for a specific purpose?
2. What details of Mary's story speak to me? What strikes me most about her words? Her actions? Her attitude?
3. How is God trying to overshadow my life? How is he present, dwelling in me? How is he asking me to bear him out into the world?
4. Have I given him my yes? If so, what has happened as a result? If not, what is holding me back?

CHAPTER TWO

"YOU HAVE A VOICE"

Elizabeth, Mother of John the Baptist

In the days of King Herod of Judea, there was a priest named Zechariah, who belonged to the priestly order of Abijah. His wife was a descendant of Aaron, and her name was Elizabeth. Both of them were righteous before God, living blamelessly according to all the commandments and regulations of the Lord. But they had no children, because Elizabeth was barren, and both were getting on in years.

Once when he was serving as priest before God and his section was on duty, he was chosen by lot, according to the custom of the priesthood, to enter the sanctuary of the Lord and offer incense. Now at the time of the incense offering, the whole assembly of the people was praying outside. Then there appeared to him an angel of the Lord, standing at the right side of the altar of incense. When Zechariah saw him, he was terrified; and fear overwhelmed him. But the angel said to him, "Do not be afraid, Zechariah, for your prayer has been heard. Your wife Elizabeth will bear you a son, and you will name him John."

After those days his wife Elizabeth conceived, and for five months she remained in seclusion. She said, "This is what the Lord has done for me when he looked favorably on me and took away the disgrace I have endured among my people."

Now the time came for Elizabeth to give birth, and she bore a son. Her neighbors and relatives heard that the Lord had shown his great mercy to her, and they rejoiced with her.

—LUKE 1:5–13, 24–25, 57–58

• • • • •

O ver the years, Elizabeth had become a woman of few words. She had taken to letting Zechariah do most of the talking in a crowd. Yet, she herself had every reason to speak on her own behalf. A daughter of Aaron, she is called. She was a daughter and likely a granddaughter and great-granddaughter of priests. Her marriage to the prominent priest Zechariah bespeaks the careful upbringing and training she received in her home. She was undoubtedly a woman of virtue, by virtue of her family heritage.

Yet, because she was also barren, childless well into the twilight years of her life, people did not always treat her with kindness, let alone deference. Clearly, the Almighty had spoken by closing her womb. Though her name means "God is an oath" or "God's abundance," a name that suggests that God keeps his promises, Elizabeth had not yet seen those abundant promises fulfilled. And in her society, being blessed with a child was the surest sign of God's faithfulness. What for her was an unfulfilled dream—a child that she longed for but could not conceive—was also reason for people to wonder if Elizabeth was really worthy of God's promises after all.

It breaks your heart a bit just to read it, doesn't it? Infertility turned the fertile ground of Elizabeth's righteousness into a barren desert of disappointment. Although she was on in years and on in wisdom and on in holiness, no one could bear witness to the fruit of her life. No matter what other good she had done, she had not borne a child.

Elizabeth was a woman who knew *what* God's promises were and believed *that* they were, but she was unable to make her body bear witness to what she believed, to bring forth the fruit that was the one sure sign of his blessing in her time and place. She was unable to do the one thing that proved beyond all doubt that her long walk of blamelessness at Zechariah's side was worth something. She had yet to bring life to God's promise.

You can imagine Elizabeth in the early years, walking fresh and confident in the calling God had placed upon her life, sure of his promises and strong of step along the path of righteousness. How many of us can look back at the hopes and dreams we had for ourselves in our younger years and not blush a bit at our own innocent naïveté? So many unexpected things change the course of our lives, and we have to adapt our hopes and dreams to those changes. There have been moments when I resented that work, when I had to wrestle my way out of bitter disappointment and hold fast to God and his promises to get me there.

Based on the birth spacing of my first four children, I used to daydream about just how big our family would be when our days of baby bearing were done. I'd count seven, then happily dream of an eighth, a little extra miracle. Yet, four times I miscarried babies I desperately longed to hold. My young heart never imagined burying a baby, then sudden secondary infertility marked by four more losses. The shifting of the dream was painful. Why would God withhold such a good thing from us?

This pain intensified, feeling like an exposed wound as I struggled to quiet my heart and find hope in my circumstances. I grew weary of the "five boys?" comments perfect strangers would aim at me when I was out and about with my sons. I had no doubt that these people had no idea of the pain their question inflicted upon me. Yet, no words came; the pain of loss and the work of holding on had a choke hold on my voice.

And so, I can picture Elizabeth averting her own gaze and hastening past the crowd outside the gates as the years got long and the hope faded. I can understand how she might have grown weary of the journey—tired of the eyes that watched her and wondered what she could possibly be hoping for, tired of the whispered questions and growing assumptions. I know that tiredness. But I know too that, in that silence, there is a hope that even if God has not answered us the way we wished, he is still good. I know that there is a reality beyond my own dreams that is eternal, a reality that God's will for me is always leading me back to him, even when it may not look like every dream of mine came true.

This hope in God's goodness is more than hope, really. It is a lifeline, as vital as our next breath. It keeps our quiet hearts going when it seems we cannot bear the looming question over our lives for one more moment. It is a hope I have often clung to in quiet conversation with God, and it is Elizabeth's hope here, as we meet her in the Gospels.

Elizabeth grew quiet in that hope. Tucked away at home, she still believed, but she was silent as Zechariah made his way into the temple. It was a once-in-a-lifetime opportunity for him to offer the prayers of the people. But what God heard was the prayer of his heart, a heart joined in love and loyalty to Elizabeth's heart. And even though she stayed hidden in silence, it was her wildly desperate hope that God's oath was true that was whispered back in the Holy of the Holies that day.

And it turned everything upside down. Zechariah, the speaker, the voice of the people, is suddenly silenced. And a new voice takes center stage, that of Elizabeth, who whispers: "This is what the Lord has done for me when he looked favorably on me and took away the disgrace I have endured among my people" (Luke 1:25). Elizabeth speaks, she who had lost her voice to the disgrace and shame, not of God, but of others— of *her* people. The very ones who were supposed to be *for* her had chosen instead to put a deadline on God's opportunity to use her, declaring her a broken promise, a blemished hope, and whispering among themselves that certainly there must be some reason why.

Maybe you are familiar with this silence. Have you too grown quiet in your hope? Have your people also marked your circumstances a disgrace? Your long waiting, your steady faith—maybe they have become solitary and lonely. Your hope lives, but your heart is quiet. If this is your story, then Elizabeth is your sister. And she has a message for you: You have a voice. You have something to say. God has promises to keep, and he wants you to proclaim them. He will silence the crowd so you can be heard when the time comes—just as he did for Elizabeth.

Elizabeth's voice rang out into a world that didn't even know anymore what it was waiting for. The whole world had grown bored and busy in waiting for its salvation. The silent void of waiting had filled with the noise of human brokenness. But strong, silent Elizabeth held hope. Her voice continues to ring out across the story of salvation. Hope is rising. Dawn is coming. Because our God keeps his oath.

And in his presence, you have a voice. You too have something vitally important to say. You are meant to testify to his faithfulness, to proclaim his blessings, to break through the world's noise with the voice of truth.

In one instant, the little bubble of hope that floated out when

Elizabeth heard the news of her own pregnancy bursts, and the words spill out. Elizabeth sheds the disgraceful shackles of lonely silence for this: "Blessed are you among women, and blessed is the fruit of your womb" (Luke 1:42). Elizabeth is the first human to publicly proclaim the Good News that God has been made man and our salvation has come! And she did so, not at the Temple gates, but right there on her doorstep, hugging her cousin. She is the first person to come in contact with Mary, with the dwelling place of God made man. And in recognizing his presence, she reflects Mary's perfect hope and fullness of grace. Mary brings Jesus to Elizabeth, and in his presence, Elizabeth gives voice to the hope we all have in him.

Can you imagine how it felt finally to release the cork on that bottle of hope? After so many long years of waiting, so many sideways glances, so many bitter days of personal disappointment and public disgrace, Elizabeth finally felt in the depth of her being that it had been true all along: God had a plan. And she was part of it. And there was a baby. And he was real, and he was there inside her, and he knew God like she did.

Who could keep from singing at that moment? The moment when God finally shows up, and you can gasp in relief and raise your hands and sing out the praise because he is an oath keeper? Elizabeth could not stop herself, either.

She declares them blessed, the two women standing there in her humble doorway, holding all of salvation history in their wombs. They are blessed because they believed God's every word. They did not let disgrace sully truth. They believed.

Elizabeth's voice cries out in triumph, her song a spark of unbridled joy turned loose upon the dark, waiting world. Her cousin's joy loosens Mary's tongue, and she joins in. Elizabeth's voice sings the verse that gives rise to the chorus, the song that will be repeated throughout salvation history: "Blessed is she who believed that there would be a fulfillment of what was spoken to her by the Lord" (Luke 1:45). Mary sings the chorus, and we are each offered the chance to sing a verse in the salvation song. Will we sing ours out with the same long-awaited joy? Will we believe long enough that, when we see God's faithfulness, praise will spring from us like a flood that had been held back for as long as it could be contained and is now set free to run its course?

This is the power of voice—of Elizabeth's voice and Mary's voice and your voice too. When we use our voice to proclaim the faithfulness of God and the wonders of his love, and when we speak and walk in obedience, our voice calls forth the voices of others.

Oh, how I want to be an Elizabeth to our world. I want to be a woman whose faith in God's promises holds no matter how long there is no visible evidence of it—a woman who uses her voice to bring hope to the weary and to rejoice with those who rejoice. I want to proclaim God's goodness and faithfulness steadily, with great joy, regardless of what the world around me looks like—because when it is darkest, that is when my voice is most needed.

Do you feel the world around you bending with heaviness these days? Do you also long to be the voice that rings with hope? It is a heart trained in righteousness that gives rise to that kind of voice. Elizabeth's hope lay in a God she knew intimately because she had long followed him in obedience and humility. Let us do the same, sisters.

Elizabeth's last words in Luke's Gospel are simple and firm. She faces the crowd that has been her shame and that wants to name her baby for her. "He is to be called John," she confidently states (Luke 1:60). She speaks out over the noise of the crowd with the confidence of righteous and obedient faith. And she declares him John, which means "God is gracious."

God's oath is real, and he is gracious and good. That is her message to all of us. And at this utterance, again a tongue is loosed and a voice called forth: that of her husband, Zechariah, who also knows that God is gracious and proclaims it to be true. Yes, after all the long waiting, God has kept his oath, and he is gracious. There is no more waiting, no more disgrace, no more silence. He is John, just as Elizabeth has spoken. Her voice has found its place.

Elizabeth speaks first in the whisper of wonder, then in the exuberant joy of seeing God's promise fulfilled, and lastly in the firm confidence of one who has been obedient and seen God keep his oath. She is the daughter-preacher of the priest and the mother-prophetess of the last prophet. She had a voice, and God had a plan for it from the beginning of time. He tried her voice in her faithful waiting and then used her voice to raise the song of salvation. Elizabeth, a woman on in years but no longer barren, was indeed blameless in God's sight and blessed because she believed. Her voice gives birth to the final prophetic voice of salvation history, to the one who prepares the way of the Lord.

~ WHO DOES HE SAY YOU ARE? ~
AN INVITATION TO LIFT YOUR VOICE

You are like Elizabeth. You too have a voice that God wants to use.

Are you still holding on to your quiet hope? Are you still tucked away in your self-imposed, silent corner? Have you endured long years of waiting and bitter disappointment? Have you waited long for grace and found only dis-grace? Have you stopped sharing your hopes and dreams with the gathering crowd and stayed back from the festivals and Temple gates? Have you begun to wonder if you even remember how to sing anymore, if you would even recognize the sound of your own voice?

Don't be afraid, sister. You will. There is a whisper and a song and a firm purpose that echoes through the generations of God's daughters. The song has been sung before you, and you are meant to sing your verse and teach others the chorus so that they may follow. Our God is gracious, and he will be so to you as he was to your sister Elizabeth.

You can believe it. The moment is coming when salvation joy and God's faithfulness will leap into reality inside of you, and you will know that, yes, it really is as he promised it would be. And then you will not be able to keep from singing out to the world. You will settle confidently into your purpose and come to know the sound of your own voice. You will loosen the tongues of your fellow prophets and break through the darkness of a world that cannot remember what it is they are waiting for.

This is your heritage and your calling.

Your voice has the power to transform individuals and communities: your family, your friends, the multitude, and the one person on your doorstep. And if you will just risk starting with a whisper, oh, what could happen!

"Fear came over all their neighbors, and all these things were talked about throughout the entire hill country of Judea" (Luke 1:65). Elizabeth's voice turned the ugly gossip of disgrace back into reverence and awe. Her voice made God's goodness the topic of conversation at the tables of her neighbors.

It started with one whispered hope. One woman gave voice to one risky thought that it might just be true that God is real and that he keeps his promises—and it grew into a chorus of yeses. Yes, it is true, and, yes, he does—and, oh, how good it is!

Maybe you have grown used to keeping hope quiet too, but maybe you feel the whisper rising. Maybe you are beginning to remember the sound of your own voice. Go ahead, whisper it. Before you know it, the singing will come and the firm confidence will be yours. Shall we sing together the song that Elizabeth has taught us? *God is gracious and keeps his promises, and blessed is she who believed every word.*

~ LET US PRAY ~

Lord God, Voice of Truth, thank you for my voice. Thank you for having given me a way to whisper grace and sing out your goodness and affirm your will with conviction.

Father, there are ways in which I have grown quiet. Some hopes and dreams in my heart are too long-awaited, too sacred to be the stuff of idle chatter. Lord, I trust your faithfulness and your goodness and your love. I offer these dreams back to you and entrust them to your care.

Heal me of the pains that have come in the waiting, God. Help me forgive the ones who should have come alongside me in my weariness, but who only added to my dis-grace in my dark days of disappointment. Speak into the depths of me that I am not a disgrace to you, Father. You are faithful, and even now you are redeeming every hard waiting and every disappointment for your purpose.

Teach me to sing again of your faithfulness, Gracious One. Open my mouth to give you praise with exuberant joy. Give me courage, Lord, to speak, to let my lips declare what I know in my inmost being: I am blessed by your love.

Thank you, Lord, for giving me a voice and a hope and a purpose, as well as blessings to proclaim. Thank you for the whisper and the shout and the simple, obedient statement, all of which are mine to sound out and are designed by your hand. Thank you for considering the sound of my voice as lovely to your ears.

Teach me to use my voice to dispel disgrace with your graciousness so that the people around me may learn to speak of your goodness. Amen.

~ Questions for Reflection ~

1. What are the hopes and dreams I have come to guard quietly in my heart? Do I still believe God is working to bring them to fruition? Am I willing to entrust those dreams to him, to trust that he will give me what he knows is best for me?

2. What are some ways that God asks me to use my voice to proclaim his goodness? Should I do so in a whisper, in a song of praise, or with firm conviction?

3. Elizabeth's name means "God's oath" or "God's abundance." How can I see that God keeps his promises and that God is abundant in my life right now? How can I give voice to those truths so as to transform people around me?

4. What is unique about my voice?

———— ⊗⊗⊗ ————

CHAPTER THREE

"YOU ARE A WITNESS"

Anna the Prophetess

When the time came for their purification according to the law
of Moses, they brought him up to Jerusalem to present him to
the Lord (as it is written in the law of the Lord, "Every firstborn
male shall be designated as holy to the Lord"), and they offered
a sacrifice according to what is said in the law of the Lord, "a
pair of turtledoves or two young pigeons."

Now there was a man in Jerusalem whose name was Simeon;
this man was righteous and devout, looking forward to the
consolation of Israel, and the Holy Spirit rested on him. It had
been revealed to him by the Holy Spirit that he would not see
death before he had seen the Lord's Messiah. Guided by the
Spirit, Simeon came into the temple; and when the parents
brought in the child Jesus, to do for him what was customary
under the law, Simeon took him in his arms and praised God....
And the child's father and mother were amazed at what was
being said about him. Then Simeon blessed them and said to
his mother Mary, "This child is destined for the falling and the
rising of many in Israel, and to be a sign that will be opposed so
that the inner thoughts of many will be revealed—and a sword
will pierce your own soul too."

There was also a prophet, Anna the daughter of Phanuel, of
the tribe of Asher. She was of a great age, having lived with her
husband seven years after her marriage, then as a widow to

the age of eighty-four. She never left the temple but worshiped there with fasting and prayer night and day. At that moment she came, and began to praise God and to speak about the child to all who were looking for the redemption of Jerusalem.

—LUKE 2:22–28, 33–38

. . . . .

I had long imagined Anna as a rather pitiful figure. In my mind's eye she was old and decrepit, wrapped in ragged cloaks, and sitting in the Temple in a kind of sad dream state, muttering prayers and utterances through eyes clouded with age. I saw her as a holy woman, yes, but not a particularly happy one.

But if we take a closer look at the details that we can glean from this short description, the picture that they reveal is altogether different from those impressions. Anna is not a woman to be pitied. She is not withering away to nothingness on the Temple floor while she slowly loses sight of who she once was. No, Anna is a woman who has lived a full life and who is still living fully, with a keen vision and a clear heart.

She is the daughter of Phanuel, of the tribe of Asher. Phanuel means "face or vision of God," and Asher means "happy or blessed." Anna too is called a "prophet," one chosen to hear and receive messages from the Lord and proclaim them to others. Anna is one who sees, who is given a glimpse of what is to come from the Lord, and who is charged to pronounce that vision to his people. She is blessed with vision of God.

We know also that at the moment she enters the biblical scene of the presentation in the Temple, she is at least eighty-four years old. We know that Anna had been married seven years and is a widow. She has lived long, and she has lived well. And we know that Anna spends her days in the Temple, in fasting and prayer. How long this has been the practice of her life, we are not told. But the words certainly hint that it has been for many long years that Anna has dedicated herself to a life of pure dependence on God. And it seems that she has gained a reputation in those years as a woman of vision, one who has the gift to see what God is up to in this world and to announce it to others.

On the surface, it might appear that we have very little in common with this elderly Jewish widow who spends her days in prayer and fasting in the Temple. Our days are usually filled with full sinks and empty bellies, people who need our attention, and floors that need to be swept. But if we take the time to scratch deeper than the surface, we can see that Anna has much to show us about who we are.

Anna is a woman of vision. She knows that something new is coming, and she lives in great hope of that coming. Because of that hope, she spends her days in the discipline of waiting on the Lord and serving his people. Anna waits publicly on the Lord and fasts from the things that would cloud her vision of his presence, so that when he reveals himself, she will be ready to make public proclamation of her grand hope.

We do not have to be so different after all, do we, friends? Which of us, no matter what the physical commitments of our days look like, wouldn't want to be known for spiritual greatness, as a woman of vision who sees clearly what God is doing among his people? And in what does that kind of ability lie, the ability to see clearly? If Anna is our guide, then it lies in a life committed to prayer, to humble service, to being sustained wholly by God, and to being willing to proclaim publicly his presence to others when it is revealed.

We live in a world today that is in need of women of vision. And we are those women, sisters. We are the new prophetesses, following in Anna's great footsteps. We are called to live the kind of life she lived, so fully focused on God that we do not miss the subtle ways that he reveals himself to our world.

We, friend, must be the ones who are paying attention, returning over and over again to the sacred and quiet things, so that if God shows up in the tiniest of forms, we will notice, just as Anna did.

The challenge of our busy days and fast-paced lives is to make the space to seek clarity of vision. And so, perhaps we should fast, not from food like Anna, but by turning away from the things that fill our calendars and our days, our ears and our eyes. Maybe the true fasting that makes both Anna and us women of vision is the fasting that makes space in our fullness, quiet in our noisiness, dependence in our capability.

Scripture tells us that Anna arrives at the Temple just as the scene of the presentation begins to unfold. Where had she been, and what had she been doing? Had Anna been at home scraping the day's lunch from the bottom of a pot, or lending a listening ear to a family member or friend in need? What prompted her to know that this was the moment that she needed to set aside whatever it was she was doing and run to her familiar, sacred space? What made Anna's heart know that God had something to show her?

We can imagine that if Anna had cultivated the discipline of going through her days in prayer, and had tuned her vision so clearly as to be always on the lookout for God's promised Messiah, then Anna's arrival at the Temple was not a mere coincidence. She came because she had been called. And she heard the call because she lived her life listening for it.

And what about you and me, sister? Are we living that life? Are we saying no to the things that overfill our lives and living fully reliant on God? Has prayer become such a part of us that it has no beginning and no end in our days—so that we live always listening for God, always looking for how he is moving? Are we detached enough from this world that, when we see he is at work and has called us to come, we do not miss the moment?

My outward life looks nothing like Anna's, but the clarity of my vision is not dependent upon the circumstances of my exterior life; rather, it is dependent upon the quality of my interior life. I become a woman of vision by living a life of prayer and fasting and by paying attention to the things of God. This is the calling of a woman of strength and courage, a woman who knows who she is because she has stripped away her reliance on other things and has allowed God to reveal her true identity. This is our calling—all of us women who live in the hope and anticipation of a Savior, and of a world that recognizes God's presence and receives it with rejoicing. We are the women of vision our world needs, friend, and we must cultivate a life that makes space for the seeing.

This constant drawing near to the Lord that Anna lives is the hallmark of a life full of hope, a life of vision that knows and recognizes God when he is present. And it must be the hallmark of our lives, so that we, like Anna, will know when our faithful God comes with saving grace, and so that we too shall be transformed.

This transformation is very likely the reason that the Anna we see in the presentation scene is very different from the woman we might have expected, based on the Gospel account of this holy widow. Yes, she is aged. She should be slow to move, even feeble. She should struggle to hear and to see clearly. But as Simeon raises the baby Jesus in benediction and blessing, Anna arrives swiftly, and with perfect clarity she perceives what it is that Simeon's words and actions signify. Anna has been made strong by the life she has lived. Her vision has been made clear and her hearing fine-tuned. She has waited in joyful hope for the coming of her Savior, and she has seen him come.

Anna stands in the Temple with Mary, our model of womanhood fully transformed in Christ. They are two women who seem completely different from one another. One is young, one old. One is newly married, one long widowed. One is holding the hope of our salvation in her hands yet hearing of her coming sorrows, and one is wearing the long years of her sorrow in her bones but going away rejoicing for having seen the Lord come.

These two lives look very different, yet they are held by the same hope, alive with the same attentiveness to God, and transformed by the same Savior who has been made present to them in the most unexpected of ways. Could we also join them? Could we stop making excuses about the external circumstances that keep us from being the women of vision we are called to be? Could we instead focus on the life of the heart, which prepares us to live in the hope that our God is going to do great things? Could we create lives of vision, in which we pay constant attention to the workings of our God among us? Could we be the ones who see what our world needs most and recognize it in the face of Christ, who so often comes to us, hidden and small? And could we be the ones who go out rejoicing, giving thanks, and proclaiming hope to the waiting ones?

Whatever it is that defines your life right now, you are a woman of vision, a woman who has the gift of seeing, because the one who is called Christ, the Messiah, has come, and he gives clarity to your hope and purpose to your vision. He makes you see the truest of truths and know the most joyful rejoicing.

~ WHO DOES HE SAY YOU ARE? ~
AN INVITATION TO SHARE YOUR HOPE

We're all waiting for something. Recently I was expressing to my therapist how my longing for another child is never satiated. I told her, because of that, I often found myself longing for a way out of my ministry to moms and babies, to know that if I chose to one day, I could walk away from it all and take up the path I'd prefer to walk.

She looked at me intently and asked, "Do you think there is anyone in this world who could do what you do with the unique compassion with which you do it?" I hesitated. I didn't want to be the one to articulate the answer. She did it for me. "No," she said, "plain and simple, no. There is no one who has the heart you do for these mamas and their babies. There is no one who longs to bring them hope like you do."

I left her office that day and made my way back home, going over the birth of this ministry in my mind—how I had seen those first mothers, bellies swollen, climbing into the backs of ambulances alone with nothing but a tiny bag carrying their personal documents. I had longed to run behind that vehicle yelling for it to stop, to climb up inside and hold their hands while their bodies rocked with the work of bringing new life into the world.

I remember the day God whispered that my longings were his and this was his dream too, and told me just to bring the women home with me—and then just hours later I found a mother on the path, carrying a sick infant. I remember how I sat with her until help came and later welcomed her into my home and administered life-saving medicines to her little one, until days passed and the worst danger was over.

The faces of babies and mothers who would have been lost without this ministry flash across my mind, and I remember how many ways I have seen him move, seen him work, in small and unexpected but very real ways. And I realize that without those quiet days of longing and sorrow by the river, where my heart learned the disciplines of praying and letting go of the things that once filled my heart in God's place, I might have missed it: how he was moving there among his people and how he wanted me to be a part of it.

The memories are a reminder of his faithfulness, of his goodness. They calm my heart's racing and settle my spirit.

I do not need a way out. I simply need to remember where my hope lies. Even the goodness of another child of my own cannot fill me with the hope I really need. And my holding on to that longing in place of dependence on God can cloud my vision and make it hard for me to see what he is about.

What if I followed Anna's example and stopped looking for a way out of dependence on God and into the fulfillment of my own longings? How much more clearly would I be able to hear the early stirrings of the Spirit? How much more quickly would I recognize his face even when it appears in unexpected ways?

Anna was not worn out by her years of waiting for God to show his face. No, instead she was strengthened by them, her hope so clear and so pure that she had no doubt about what she was seeing the moment she walked into the scene of Simeon holding out a tiny baby—who by all accounts looked just like all the other tiny babies he held in the Temple. Anna's was a hope refined by prayer and by letting go of her own expectations so as to do the work of the Lord. Anna was a woman with the vision to know the difference between expectant hope and hope in her own expectations.

Are you that kind of woman, friend? I confess I have often not been. Not only in the big hopes and dreams and expectations, like having another child, but even in the small details of my everyday life, I often get trapped by own expectations. I forget that my hope is not that things will go as I planned, but that the Lord will make himself known, in the faces of my husband and children, in the unexpected joys of family life that pop up right in the middle of our messy chaos, in the ways he provides for me and shows me his tender care in the most detailed ways.

To be a woman who recognizes God because she has learned to hope only in him, I first have to be a woman like Anna, a woman of prayer and fasting, a woman from whom thanksgiving flows, a woman who speaks of the Lord with great joy to those waiting to know him. Anna doesn't just recognize Jesus at that moment in the Temple, but she is transformed by the recognition. She lets the unexpected blessing of the babe in Simeon's arms and the glory glowing on his face turn her heart to rejoicing. Her hope blossoms into joy and thanksgiving in the presence of the Messiah, and she shares it with those who are waiting with uncertainty, unsure of what they are looking for.

How many people in your life are like the ones that Anna proclaimed the presence of Christ to that day? People who are searching, hoping, and waiting for something but unable to define just what it is they are waiting for? Where will you find the courage to tell them with great joy that the one thing that satisfies all their searching, the One to fulfill their hope, has come, is here now, and they can rejoice with you?

The courage to live the call to share Jesus with others comes from a hope that gives way to the discipline of prayer. Prayer inspires a life of joyful dependence on the Lord, which allows us to see and recognize him at work in the most surprising of ways. And from a heart focused on God blossoms the thanksgiving that overflows into sharing Christ with a waiting world.

This is the call of the seer, the prophetess. This is our call, friends. It wasn't strange for the Jews in the Temple to receive Anna as a woman of vision, because women who had come before her had set the precedent. And we do not have to shy away from being women of vision, because we have Anna as our example and our guide. We, like her, have Mary too to show us what a woman's heart can look like when it has fully embraced life with Christ. Their examples are rich with fodder for our own transformations, friends. Let us take their stories to heart. Let us allow ourselves to be defined, not by the way we live on the outside, but by who we are on the inside. Let us cultivate lives of prayer and purpose, of grand hopes and humble graces. Let us live fully alive and aware, prepared to see God work and to proclaim his goodness.

Our world is one that is breaking from pain and sin in every direction we look, it seems. But we do not have to give up hope, sister, because we are women who see. If we will set our hearts on the discipline of prayer and give up the things that keep us from living wholly dependent on him, we will see God in action, recognize him at work, and have the courage to go out and proclaim his presence with great rejoicing. Our homes, our towns, and our world need us to be women of vision. They need us to know when God is stirring and to show up to witness his coming. They need us to run out rejoicing because we have hoped in him and seen our hopes confirmed. Our world is waiting for its prophetesses. My sister, let us answer that call.

~ Let Us Pray ~

Dear Jesus, surprising Savior, I want to be a woman of vision, a woman who sees you in action, recognizes your presence, and has the courage to offer the hope you bring to those waiting to know you. Help me, Lord, to become this woman.

Give me the grace to give up the things that cloud my heart and that keep me from a hope wholly dependent on you. Help me to recognize the surprising ways you speak. Teach me to sense with confidence your hand at work. Give me the gift of a disciplined heart, Lord, so that I can have clear vision, know my purpose, and live it fully. Teach me to rejoice with a thanksgiving that becomes a proclamation of your presence to those around me.

Make me, Lord, a prophetess, whose life is spent looking for you to move, listening intently to your voice, and seeing you at work. Make me a woman who hopes in you above all else and whose hope is forever renewed by seeing you present in my life in the most unexpected ways. Give me a heart that goes out rejoicing and proclaiming your praise to the hearts in my midst who are still waiting to know you.

Make me a woman of vision, God, with a heart that sees and a clear purpose to proclaim you. I am waiting, Lord, with a hope that can be satisfied only in you. Amen.

~ Questions for Reflection ~

1. How am I cultivating a life of prayer and spiritual discipline? What are the obstacles I face in living a life of prayer?
2. What are the things in my life that fill me, distract me, and prevent me from living wholly dependent on God?
3. How is God at work in my life in small and surprising ways? Am I paying attention to Christ present in my everyday life?
4. Have I ever wished for the courage to proclaim Christ to others in my life? This longing is not without purpose. How might I begin to cultivate that courage?

CHAPTER FOUR

"You Bear No Shame"
The Woman of Samaria

So he came to a Samaritan city called Sychar, near the plot of ground that Jacob had given to his son Joseph. Jacob's well was there, and Jesus, tired out by his journey, was sitting by the well. It was about noon.

A Samaritan woman came to draw water, and Jesus said to her, "Give me a drink." (His disciples had gone to the city to buy food.) The Samaritan woman said to him, "How is it that you, a Jew, ask a drink of me, a woman of Samaria?" (Jews do not share things in common with Samaritans.) Jesus answered her, "If you knew the gift of God, and who it is that is saying to you, 'Give me a drink,' you would have asked him, and he would have given you living water." The woman said to him, "Sir, you have no bucket, and the well is deep. Where do you get that living water? Are you greater than our ancestor Jacob, who gave us the well, and with his sons and his flocks drank from it?" Jesus said to her, "Everyone who drinks of this water will be thirsty again, but those who drink of the water that I will give them will never be thirsty. The water that I will give will become in them a spring of water gushing up to eternal life." The woman said to him, "Sir, give me this water, so that I may never be thirsty or have to keep coming here to draw water."

Jesus said to her, "Go, call your husband, and come back." The woman answered him, "I have no husband." Jesus said to her,

"You are right in saying, 'I have no husband'; for you have had five husbands, and the one you have now is not your husband. What you have said is true!" The woman said to him, "Sir, I see that you are a prophet. Our ancestors worshiped on this mountain, but you say that the place where people must worship is in Jerusalem." Jesus said to her, "Woman, believe me, the hour is coming when you will worship the Father neither on this mountain nor in Jerusalem. You worship what you do not know; we worship what we know, for salvation is from the Jews. But the hour is coming, and is now here, when the true worshipers will worship the Father in spirit and truth, for the Father seeks such as these to worship him. God is spirit, and those who worship him must worship in spirit and truth." The woman said to him, "I know that the Messiah is coming" (who is called Christ). "When he comes, he will proclaim all things to us." Jesus said to her, "I am he, the one who is speaking to you."

—JOHN 4:5–26

· · · · ·

The heat of the noonday sun in a desert land is deadly exhausting. People wake early and get their work done ahead of its rise to avoid the piercing heat of high noon. By the time the sun is baking the earth and parching bodies, people are retreating to their homes to rest from the morning's work. The food has been cooked, the clothes washed, the fields watered.

But the Gospels tell us a story about a weary Jesus who meets a Samaritan woman at the well at high noon. She arrives with her jars to draw water from the community well at the time of day when everyone else is retreating—instead of in the busy morning time when the chatter is lively and there are people to greet and stories to share. No, she is late to her task because she has waited until the crowds have long filtered away and been about their work.

She carries her burning thirst to the well at a time of day when she can bear her shame alone, without the threat of attention. She is weary of the burden she bears, her dry thirst for a better way, and the burning sting of shame on her face. And she doesn't expect to find a man sitting there in the shadows.

But there he is.

He too was weary, weary from watching the ones he came to save labor under a burden he had come to bear for them. He sat in the shadow of the well that day, weary for her and weary with her, and, out of love for her, feeling the dustiness of dry lips and the scratch of a thirsty tongue on his mouth's roof. His eyes stung with the drip of salty sweat and tears of redemption as he turned and spoke.

I wonder if she was able to conceal her incredulity or if she actually jumped a bit when his voice broke the silence, her awkward fumbling and skirting around his presence halted by his undivided, unafraid, and seemingly sudden attention.

His first words to her are a request: "Give me a drink." In speaking to her, he crosses the lines of that time and place. Men did not speak to women. Jews did not speak to Samaritans. But Jesus walks a different way—he is the Way. And in this way, the Savior speaks to sinners—and what he speaks is salvation.

Oh, how many lines do we try to draw to keep this Jesus at a distance? How often do we answer along with the Samaritan woman, "How can you be asking me for something? Don't you know who I am, Lord?" *I am the other, the one so not like you. You should not come near me.* We assume that our humanity and our sin are obstacles to Jesus, when, in fact, he has come to the place where we are and waited for us just so he can blow away the lines the world has drawn in the dust, and all the lines we ourselves have drawn too, with the breath of mercy.

"Sir," she addresses him—a term of deference she uses as she frantically tries to make sense of this unexpected turn of events. And yet, there is a hint that she knows that this man has something important to say to her, that she is stalling and stammering because she feels the tickle of the Spirit on her sunbaked skin and parched soul.

She questions him with incredulity and probing uncertainty: "Why are you speaking to me? What do you want from me?" Because all the men she has known have wanted something. They have engaged her only to take something from her. They have left her drawing from the dregs in the scorching heat, and who can blame her for being a little cynical?

However, what Jesus wants is not to ask but to offer. He has what she needs to quit the burning shame that leaves her parched and weary. He has life to give her. When he makes such an offer, she is not ready to believe him just yet. She knows how wells work, especially this well, the well that holds sacred space among her people. Is this Jewish man really saying he has better water to offer than the water that has been held sacred by her ancestors and her family for generations?

I wonder if the questions were simply a way to buy her time to consider this man for a moment—this man who breaks all the rules and who says the strangest things. Maybe she needed a minute to decide what her next step would be. But instead, all she can think of is the thought of never being thirsty again. It compels her beyond a rational response, even beyond propriety.

He never really answers her questions, yet she forgets all the shame that bound her, all the fear that kept her questioning from a safe distance. He has life-giving water to offer—water that will "become in [her] a spring of water gushing up to eternal life" so that she "may never be thirsty" (John 4:13–14). And she wants that. Oh, how she wants to drink freely, gulp greedily, and not be thirsty! How she longs to be free of the need that binds her to the kind of love that never slakes her deepest thirst. How she longs to leave behind the shame that she lays upon her own shoulders each day as she comes to draw for herself the bit she needs to survive, arriving in the late hours, when the watching eyes of the righteous have turned to their work and only the weary draw near to the well.

And we all echo it with her, don't we? "Give me this water, so that I may never be thirsty or have to keep coming here." So I won't have to feel the dust of the earth clinging to my lips, its grit on my tongue. So I won't find my soul so dry and parched and weary from looking for love that I am drawn over and over again into the seedy substitutes that only leave me standing exposed to the scorching rays of sin. So I won't spend my days in hiding, shouldering my shame and my need, and making my way into the light only when I am assured that I will not be seen. Yes, give us this water, good Sir. We are weary and we are thirsty, and we do not want to come to this place again.

I have known her weariness. I have known the burning shame of sin and of looking to be filled by all the wrong things. Which of us hasn't, friends? Which of us has not known the moment of coming to Jesus so parched that we will break all the rules to get the life we know he longs to pour into us. We will insist and beg and plead that he come to our aid.

So urgent is the need of this Samaritan woman, so pressing the call to freedom, that she is greedy for it. There is an insistence, a demand almost, in her voice: "Give me this water." Fix it, Lord—quickly. Take away the uncomfortable, and give me what I want. It is whispered under the surface of her urging. And it is under ours too, is it not? We see what Jesus has to offer, and we want a way out of our misery. And we want it now. We are greedy for relief.

But Jesus is a slow and patient man, just as he is a slow and patient God. He is a God who chooses transformation over quick fixes and full freedom over halfhearted embraces. So he invites this woman into an intimacy that pierces as it purges. He points out the places inside her that will keep her always thirsty, no matter how much water he pours into her. Life cannot spring from death, and our Jesus cares about our slowly dying souls more than he cares about our public appearance. He wants to heal us not only from the outside shame that keeps us baking in the public glare, but from the deep, personal shame that keeps us gingerly sidestepping our real wounds while we wither within.

So he stares down her insistence with love. And he opens the bandages she wears over her sin and shame and looks closely at the wounds. She is revealed—uncomfortably, intimately seen by this man she never meant to meet. "Go, call your husband" is the command with which he rebuts her insistence.

Oh, haven't we been there? We too have wanted God to do something for us, anything to take away the pain and fix our mess, to be saved and done, when suddenly he stares down the real need and draws it into the light. I wonder how long it took her to respond, to gather herself from the gut punch of his words and the realization that the conversation wasn't going her way. I wonder how deep the sigh was, and if it felt more like a groan when she finally figured that it was worth telling him the truth.

"I have no husband," she clips out. It is a curt answer given to protect herself from the probing, to keep her shame hidden and her wounds bandaged even as they wept and begged for healing.

Jesus is not convinced or put off by easy, first answers, by our cues to go no further. He wants to get to the deepest parts of us. Just as this woman thirsts so desperately that she insists on her relief through living water, he is so thirsty for our freedom that he insists on the whole freeing truth. He is not content to fill us and leave us, slaked but sinful, bandaged but in bondage to shame. So he probes right into the heart of the deepest, darkest places of our souls, and he loves them right into the light. "You are right in saying, 'I have no husband'; for you have had five husbands, and the one you have now is not your husband. What you have said is true!" Jesus indicates with knowing patience that what she has said is true, but not the whole truth.

He stands right here in front of you with the same knowing insistence. He longs for your healing, your freedom, but he will not give you only half of what you need. He will not treat just the thirsty symptoms of your sin and leave you to walk in shame. He has fixed his gaze on your heart, and he sees the deepest parts of you that need him. Tell him the truth, the whole truth. Let him see all of you, even the parts that have not seen the light for so long, the parts that you shroud and shelter in secret. He thirsts for you like you thirst for him. There is freedom waiting for you. You do not have to come to this place again. But he can't heal what you won't let him touch.

It's likely that you haven't had five husbands. Maybe you've had other idols that have muddied the waters of your faith and left you making a practice of avoiding the truth. Whatever it is that keeps you hiding from the Lord and rebuffing him when he draws near, that is the thing you must confess and bear before him if what you desire is never to bake under the heat of shame again.

Sin breeds shame. But Jesus offers the woman the remedy— "Spirit and truth." The hour is coming, he tells her, when we will set aside our sin and our shame and our age-old ways of assuaging them with a bit of water only to find our throats burning again in short time. The moment is coming when they will be remedied all together, when the water will flow that never stops giving us life. And the source of that water is the Spirit and the truth that set us free from sin and shame.

And he is crossing all the boundaries of this day and age too, to draw near to you and me and offer us the same relief: Spirit and truth. When we tell the truth about who we are and who we have been, the Spirit can move in us. The confession of our sin makes space for freedom. The slow exhale of what was once hidden invites the wind of the Spirit to blow. And on the wind, the saving grace of the Messiah rides.

It's as simple as it sounds in Scripture, an exchange so humble and matter-of-fact that it seems weightless. She believes there is a Messiah. She believes someone is coming to save her from the mess she has just confessed. She sees that there is something different in this man. He is no longer simply "sir" but "prophet"—truth teller. And then he reveals that he is the source of the other half of the remedy too: he doesn't just have the truth of the prophets, but he has the Spirit too. Could he be the Messiah?

She accepts it readily, with the same quickness with which she demanded the water he had to offer. The truth has settled on her fully, and she is as thirsty for real freedom as she was for the idea of living water. She needs no further explanation or discourse. She simply leaves behind the water jar. She leaves the object and the place that contained what life she could draw for herself from the dregs in order to keep going, even as her sin and her shame baked her dry again and again.

This woman, who had come to the well bearing so much shame, goes out announcing Jesus's presence to her people. She tells them how he knew all that she had done, just as they too had known all that she had done. But she shouts it out in a newfound freedom, not afraid to remind them of who she has been, because she knows who she is now. She knows that her encounter with Christ has freed her. She has confessed and drawn near and been offered a new life in which she bears no shame. And she embraces it fully.

In that embrace, she takes up the same work of all the righteous women we have already seen, that of Anna and Elizabeth, and of Woman herself: Mary. This woman whose life has been lived in anything but righteousness according to Jewish law becomes their equal, their sister. And she shares in their work of professing Jesus to all she meets, announcing the coming of a Savior. In the eyes of the Lord, nothing in her past prohibits her from taking up her place at their sides.

~ WHO DOES HE SAY YOU ARE? ~
AN INVITATION TO DRINK DEEPLY

And you, sister? Are you ready to take up your place too? Because Jesus is here, the one who offers us both Spirit and truth. He is the one who can wash away your sin and cover your shame. He is the one who can give you life. Are you ready to set down the water jar you've been carrying in the shadows? Are you ready to stop drawing up from the dregs and to instead drink from the source? Go ahead. Set it down. Feel your hands relax their grasp. Lick your dusty lips for the last time.

And drink deep of him. Yes, this is him—the Messiah. He has come not just to take away your sin, but to erase your shame too. No more shadows, no more noonday sun—you do not have to come here again. You have confessed the truth, and you have believed the Spirit. And you are free.

Now run to the city and tell the Good News. You have met a man who has told you all that you have ever done! And now you are free from your secrets and free from your hiding because the truth was told, the Spirit moved, and the Messiah is come! Your salvation is won. Not only can you return to face the townspeople, but you can lead the way back to him by your testimony. Your sin has been forgiven, and you bear no shame.

~ LET US PRAY ~

O Jesus, Prophet, Messiah, help me. I am tired of this daily journey to the well of self-satisfaction. I am tired of the weight of sin and the shadows of shame. I am tired of being burned by the heat of desire and of thirsting for real, life-giving love.

You have the water I need. You are the life I long for. You are the source from which my freedom flows. And you draw near and offer yourself to me. I want you, Jesus. I want so badly to be "fixed," to be saved. I am greedy and insistent, so ready to be done with this life of idols and false ideologies and with lusting after the wrong things. I'm so ready that I want to skip the step that costs me something. I want to run to you and leave it all behind. But I'm still carrying my jar.

I'm still holding it close to my chest—the thing that relieves me when the sin and the shame are too much to bear. And I don't want to face the truth. Because the truth about me is the ugly, sad truth of a sinner's heart. But you already know my story. You already see the whole truth. I have only to confess it to you to find the freedom I desire.

Hear me, Lord, now. I give you my deepest secrets and my most painful truths. I step out of the shadows into the light of your truth. Here it is, Sir. I have made a mess of my life, and I need a Savior. And I believe that you are he.

I say it today like I am saying it for the first time. I say it with the faith of the woman at the well. I believe that you are the Savior, and I want to worship in Spirit and in truth. Give me the water of life. I will set down my jar and take up my mission, set down my shame and take up my salvation, set aside my sinful ways to walk with you.

Lead me, Lord, to new life. Amen.

~ Questions for Reflection ~

1. Is shame keeping me from experiencing true community right now? In what ways am I hiding?

2. What are the things I use to satisfy myself instead of seeking Christ?

3. What do I need to tell the truth about in order to experience full freedom in Christ? What would Jesus see in me if he were standing before me now?

4. Have I confessed my sins? Do I know that I am forgiven, yet am I still holding on to shame? How can I embrace the fact of my forgiveness and step back into the light? (If you aren't sure, consider making an appointment with your pastor.)

CHAPTER FIVE

"You Are Known"

The Hemorrhaging Woman

A large crowd followed him and pressed in on him. Now there was a woman who had been suffering from hemorrhages for twelve years. She had endured much under many physicians, and had spent all that she had; and she was no better, but rather grew worse. She had heard about Jesus, and came up behind him in the crowd and touched his cloak, for she said, "If I but touch his clothes, I will be made well." Immediately her hemorrhage stopped; and she felt in her body that she was healed of her disease. Immediately aware that power had gone forth from him, Jesus turned about in the crowd and said, "Who touched my clothes?" And his disciples said to him, "You see the crowd pressing in on you; how can you say, 'Who touched me?'" He looked all around to see who had done it. But the woman, knowing what had happened to her, came in fear and trembling, fell down before him, and told him the whole truth. He said to her, "Daughter, your faith has made you well; go in peace, and be healed of your disease."

—MARK 5:24–34

• • • • •

There must have been something special about that day, some way that the spark of Jesus's divinity burned just a little bit brighter, more perceptibly. He certainly was attracting a crowd.

Had she noticed him first, or was she drawn with curiosity to the noise and bustle? I wonder if she had waited for this moment, having heard about Jesus and his healing power. Perhaps she had promised herself that if he ever passed her way, she would not let the opportunity pass by, but she would muster the courage to approach him and beg him for a healing.

This woman spent all her time on the outskirts, the margins, because she was unclean. She had grown used to avoiding crowds by now, places where she could easily get bumped or shoved and come into contact with someone. She had learned to hide away from the gathering places and the throngs and slink through the world unclean and unknown, living on the margins.

A disease had wracked her body for twelve long years. It made her hemorrhage from within, constantly bleeding out the life-giving thing she needed to be whole. She was, I am sure, weak and wounded from such pain year after year.

As if that weren't enough, the same disease that leaked life right out of her made her someone invisible, living on the outskirts of her community and society because she was "unclean." She was a castaway on an island of lonely isolation, unseen by the people around her even though she lived there in plain sight every day. Yes, perhaps she had taken to the shadows and the tucked-away places because being declared "unclean" was enough; she did not need to be reminded of her uncleanness by the averted glances and the slight shifts away from her.

I bet that you, like me, have known what it is like to be the invisible one in your own community, to be so wary of the judgmental glances and the avoidance maneuvers of others that you find it easier just to steer clear altogether. Whether you are the young mother with the screaming little one consigned to the back of church every Sunday, or the woman enduring incredible hardship and unable to face the judgmental glances of the ones who see imperfection as a disease, you are not alone. We have all been the invisible ones in our community at one time or other. Perhaps you have felt the judgment of being declared "unclean" and have sat in the shadows of your church, your neighborhood, or community. If you have lived that invisibility, then you know well how it can feel as if it bleeds the life right out of you. To be the one that people want to avoid can be a heavy burden.

But it can also birth a new kind of hope in us, an insight into what truly matters. We all long to be known, and it can be easy to hope that, by being received with affirmation and approval by the people around us, we will feel fulfilled. But there is no human affirmation that will meet our deepest need of being known. Time spent in loneliness and isolation can refine our hearts and teach us to look to the only One who truly knows us, the only One whose affirmation can fully satisfy us.

Maybe you can't imagine what it would be like to hemorrhage physically for twelve years with no cure to be found, but I bet you know all too well what it feels like to be hemorrhaging on the inside—all the life and joy and goodness that bring life to your soul pouring right out through a gaping wound that you just can't seem to heal. I know how grief can tear a hole in your heart and leave you bleeding all that you once hoped for right out of you. There is no instrument to cauterize that kind of heart wound.

It doesn't matter what your wound is, whether you would call it big or small, whether it is public or completely private—we all know the pain of bleeding out the very things we wish we could keep pumping through our souls. We know the pain of leaking love and grace and goodness, when all we want is to send them down to the deepest parts of our hearts to keep them beating strongly.

We've all got an open wound that needs healing, don't we? A wound that continues to bleed no matter how we try to treat it ourselves? Aren't we all really hemorrhaging women, banged and bruised and bleeding from trying to live in a harsh world where our tender hearts get pricked so often that we've kind of gotten used to the pain?

No one knew why the woman in this story kept bleeding. No one knew how to help her. No one knew what to do for her. And over time, no one knew her at all. Do you find yourself in that place? Bearing a pain that no one fully understands, so that no one fully knows what to do with you? And after enough time passes, it begins to seem that no one really knows you at all. You skim the outskirts of your own community, your own family, your own life, hide from the places where people gather, and learn to accept that you will never be fully healed, fully known, or fully accepted again.

This self-protective stance is so common, friends. I have often chosen to cocoon myself away because my hurting heart just could not risk brushing up against whatever would cause me more pain. Sometimes it's just easier to go it alone, isn't it? When we are surrounded by all the hustle and bustle, sometimes we prefer to retreat into the safety of isolation. Maybe we are bleeding on the inside, but at least we are safe from further harm. We are like the hemorrhaging woman, who had learned to hide herself away and stay unknown.

But on this one day, something suddenly draws her out, an irresistible force drawing her toward Love himself. I wonder if she knew, if she felt it deep in her bones, that this was her day. Or did she just risk it all because she had nothing to lose? Either way, she chose well. Her action plan to find her way to healing stands as an example to all who have known her isolation. She does not take the great risk of seeking human healing or approval; she doesn't merely reach out to a famous doctor as he passes by, or seek out someone who has the authority to take away her stigma of being "unclean" and return her to a better social status. No, she reaches out for the Savior, for Jesus passing there in her midst.

Who are you reaching out to, friend, to pull you from your invisibility and to truly love you? Who are you looking to for life-giving affirmation, to know you and call you back to community? Let us follow the example of our sister and reach out to the only One who can truly offer us the healing we need. The Savior is passing by, and his power to heal us is at the ready. If we are to reach, let us reach only for him, like the hemorrhaging woman of the Gospel.

She stepped out into the crowd and reached out for the first time in years. The Savior passed by, focused on his way to do a healing work, and she knew and believed in that power. She longed for just a little piece of it, not enough even to be noticed, just enough to dry up her leaking life and give her new hope. She longed to be healed. But she never dared hope for more than that. She never dared to dream that she would be seen, that she would be known again.

She pushes her way into the jostling crowd, hoping to stay unnoticed, to just reach out and brush the hem of the healer, to steal what she thinks she does not merit. A long unknown outcast, she hopes to stay hidden and yet be made whole.

Have you been there too? Have you been the one who knew how desperately she needed to be healed, who knew that Jesus was the one to do it, and who at the same time hoped that the healing would come without your being noticed, without your having to really be seen or known by him who heals?

It is a strange dichotomy, this feeling, but we are not alone in it. Oh, how many of us are both drawn to and yet terrified of this Jesus! How many of us were once known by him and now find ourselves far away! We long to draw near once again, yet we want to do so secretly, still avoiding the intimacy of his gaze. Many of us are hurting and wounded and bleeding so badly from wounds, self-inflicted from sin or meted out by life's battles in a broken world, that we've learned to be invisible in the crowds. We avoid the big groups, the churches, and the programs promising us things we know are not ours—joy, freedom, friendship. We have learned to avoid true contact with our God for fear that his gaze would melt us wide open, and we would bleed out the last life we have in us. That self-protective stance that keeps us safe from the judgmental glances and the feeling of invisibility in community also becomes the way we approach God. We want him, we reach for him, but we are just a little frightened to be fully known by him, to be really seen, to be called out of the shadows of our hiding and into the light of his love.

But our Jesus is not just a God of healing who zaps us from afar and waits for us to realize we've been healed. He heals with spit and dirt and touch. He heals with intimacy. He heals by reminding us that we are completely known, and completely loved. If we can muster just enough courage to reach out our fingertips, he will turn to find us, see us, and remind us who we are in him. He stops the hemorrhaging of our hearts with spiritual power, yes, but he sews up the wound with the power of being fully known and accepted. He won't heal us and then leave us cowering in the shadows of invisibility. No, he calls us to him so that we can be both healed and transformed. And the cause of our transformation is being fully known by him—and in turn allowing ourselves to find our acceptance and our worth in his merciful eyes, rather than in any human affirmation.

That woman, bleeding and wounded, makes her way through the crowds pressing in around Jesus, telling herself that she won't get too close, not close enough to be noticed, just enough to brush her fingertips against his hem, believing that any contact with him will be enough to bring about a miracle. She doesn't dare desire more than that—just a chance, flyby healing. There's no need for him to notice her at all.

It would seem as if Jesus might actually be grateful for her willingness to do this the easy way. He is laser-focused in that moment, already emanating with purpose as he walks toward the home of a little girl he knows he will raise from the dead. There is hurry in his step as the crowds press in around him. The desert heat burns and the dust kicks up, and the Savior is on his way to save.

So it would have been perfectly normal for him to let that release of power go unnoticed. He could have let her be secretly healed with that simple swipe of his hem. But Jesus knows about the way we bleed when we are wounded, and he knows that drying up the blood is not the thing that makes us whole again. He'll close our wounds, but then he'll turn straight toward us and call us back to the land of the living—out of the shadows and the hidden places we've learned to live in while we bled, and into the place we are known again, recognized, seen.

He turns, feeling the power leave him, and looks for her. It's not the healing he wants to account for when he turns and asks, "Who touched my clothes?" (Mark 5:30). It's the person. He wants to assure this woman, now healed, that she is not an aside to the real healing about to happen, that he didn't just have an overflow of power to dole out at that moment, but that he sees her, he knows her, and he healed her in love because she dared to believe he would.

~ WHO DOES HE SAY YOU ARE? ~
AN INVITATION TO BE NOTICED

How often have you been the woman who believed that Jesus could do great things, but forgot how much he longs to do more than just save you, how much he wants to know you singularly, with all that you have and are? He does not want to offer you a passing brush in a crowd of adoring Christians or a side of power to go with all your pain. No, Jesus sees the places where life has left you wounded and bleeding out the good stuff, where you have become invisible and unknown, and he not only longs to stop the hemorrhage but to turn and look you square in the face, to know you fully and see you completely.

I approach that reality like the woman in this story, trembling and afraid. I'm worried I have been too bold with my Lord, with my desperate faith. I'm worried I have offended him with the great risk I took in my neediness. Yes, it pains me to need the Lord as much as I do—to be the one who grabs at him in the crowd because, without him, I am without hope of ever being fully seen and fully known.

Do you know this fear, friend? Do you fear that the Lord is about healing, noticing, loving, only *others*? Do you feel a bit like the unknown daughter who just lurks around the kingdom, only daring to come out of the shadows when she desperately needs something, then feeling guilty for needing it in the first place? Do you feel like the one who has battled her pain and her woundedness for so long that no one even sees her anymore?

Do you feel that you have become invisible right there in plain sight of your own community? Do you wonder if maybe the best the Savior has to offer is for the people who need it more, who deserve it more, and that you're just meant to sneak by unnoticed in the crowd—believing in him, seeking him, but without expecting any real connection with him?

Oh, how I get that. I've been that woman. I am her, every day. But this is not our Jesus, friend. He doesn't "do" aloof; disconnection is not available to him. He is your Creator and maker, your healer and your Redeemer. He is your father, brother, and friend, the lover of your soul. This is our God.

He doesn't just do the "God stuff," doling out miracles to the deserving ones and occasionally patting one of the ordinary ones on the head as he passes by. He is a God who sees every one of us, who welcomes our need, who identifies us by our faith. He is a God who seeks us out in a crowd, turns to us, and invites us to identify ourselves in him.

And what happens when we do step forward and let him see us? He reminds us how deeply we are known. When we approach him, fall down before him, and tell him the whole truth about who we are, he lifts us up and looks deep into our faces, already so familiar to him, because he knows, he has always known, fully who we are.

Do you know what he says? He calls us daughters. He says we are beloved, his, known by the heart of the Father. He grafts us back into the family, calling us out of the shadows of our wounds and into the life-giving love of our God. He stops our bleeding, heals us, and makes us known again.

He does this because our faith is no small faith, friend. It is the faith of the ones who dare to chase after Jesus even when they are uncertain whether they deserve him. It is the faith of the ones who have long hidden from family, friends, and community, but who dare to approach their Lord and their God. It is the faith of the ones who have been bloodied and burdened by this life but who dare to hope for healing.

This is a faith worth more than a passing salvation. This is a faith worth seeing, worth recognizing. This is a faith Jesus calls out and brings to the light. Because, you, friend, are not only healed by his loving touch, but you are known. You are more than a face in the crowd. You are daughter, beloved, friend. You are fully known, seen, and loved. And because of that, you can "go in peace, and be healed of your disease."

You walk away from his gaze, no longer bleeding life out, but pumping it from within. You walk away no longer a hidden outcast, but a beloved friend who has been identified by her Lord and Savior. And you have been given a new identity. You are known by him and so you are once again fully alive, whole, out of the shadows, and walking in the light.

All of us are reaching, hoping, to get just a bit of him, but let us remember that he has already sent his power out to heal our hearts, and he has turned and looked fully upon us. He has given us a new hope born of faith, a new life born of being known. Let's step out of the shadows, sister, and remember what it is to live as women known and loved and fully free because our God has looked upon us.

~ LET US PRAY ~

Lord, healer of my heart, I am not sure when it began, the slow hemorrhaging of my soul. A nick here, a wound there, and before I knew it, a tiredness took over, and life was leaking away from me faster than I could plug up the holes. The shadows were easier—they offered shade from the glaring heat of my pain, and they allowed me to pretend that hiding was my choice, that I preferred to be alone and unknown, that there I felt safe.

But in your presence, Jesus, I can't resist having faith that you are the way back to my wholeness. I'm drawing near, Lord, reaching out for you, hoping for just a little of your love to get me through this pain, for enough healing to make life livable. I'm not asking for all of you. I'm not asking to be seen, to be known, to find my way back out of the shadows. I'm believing just enough to risk reaching for your passing touch.

Jesus, you don't deal in half-love and brush-by healing. My hemorrhaging heart is all yours, and you know every little cracked part and open wound. It is in that intimate knowing that I am healed—not in my ability to stretch and grab hold of you, but in your willingness to turn and seek me out in my reaching, to draw near and see my face. It is in being known—in being loved, in being yours—that I am made whole again.

Today I ask you for the courage of my sister, this other hemorrhaging woman, who, when you asked who had reached for you, stepped out of the shadows of her woundedness and allowed herself to be known, to be seen, and to be fully healed. Give me the faith that steps into the light, looks you in the face, and knows that, in intimacy with you, I am made whole. Let me embrace being known by you, my Lord and my God. Amen.

~ QUESTIONS FOR REFLECTION ~

1. In what ways am I hiding from God, from community? What are the wounds I experience that make me feel like an outsider?

2. When was the last time I felt God notice me? How did this make me feel? In what ways am I still keeping my distance from him?

3. What would it mean to allow Jesus to know me fully? How do I feel about Jesus calling me into a deeper and more sincere kind of intimacy with him?

4. What one step can I take to respond in faith to Jesus's question, "Who touched me?" How can I step closer to him and into a more genuine relationship with him?

CHAPTER SIX

"You Are Restored"

The Woman Caught in Adultery

Early in the morning [Jesus] came again to the temple. All the
people came to him and he sat down and began to teach them.
The scribes and the Pharisees brought a woman who had been
caught in adultery; and making her stand before all of them,
they said to him, "Teacher, this woman was caught in the very
act of committing adultery. Now in the law Moses commanded
us to stone such women. Now what do you say?" They said this
to test him, so that they might have some charge to bring against
him. Jesus bent down and wrote with his finger on the ground.
When they kept on questioning him, he straightened up and
said to them, "Let anyone among you who is without sin be the
first to throw a stone at her." And once again he bent down and
wrote on the ground. When they heard it, they went away, one
by one, beginning with the elders; and Jesus was left alone with
the woman standing before him. Jesus straightened up and said
to her, "Woman, where are they? Has no one condemned you?"
She said, "No one, sir." And Jesus said, "Neither do I condemn
you. Go your way, and from now on do not sin again."

—JOHN 8:2–11

· · · · ·

S he was caught "in the very act," they say. Her guilt was certain. She had been found in the very act of adultery. I can only imagine what exactly that might look like, but I know one thing: it wasn't pretty. And she was certainly ashamed, embarrassed, and horrified. Yes, she would have been horrified at what was to come next, but no doubt too at what already had been done, at the ripping open of the veil that hid her sin, and at having her shame dragged out into the city streets for all to see. She was a certain sinner, and now she was fully exposed and utterly vulnerable to the judgment that had been pronounced.

How much I am like her, bowing to the shame of my sin when I am discovered, when my own heart stands accusing me, dragging me through the dirt with nothing but my tears to cover the naked vulnerability that it is to be a sinner found out, a victim of her own fatal flaw.

My sin may not be adultery. Yours may be. It matters not where we were and what we were doing when the door to our heart burst open, the light poured in, and we sat dumbfounded in the glare, terrified to realize that the truth had been told, that there was no more game to be played. Whatever the wrong was that dragged us out of the darkness and left us exposed and naked in certain guilt, in the end, we all end up in the same position—bowed low and kissing the dirt, waiting for the stones we know we deserve to be cast.

I wonder what this woman, this certain sinner like you and me, did when they threw her at Jesus's feet and raised their stone-filled fists. Did she raise her arms to protect her face and head? Did she spit and kick and wriggle and squirm to fight her way out of the guilty verdict? The Scripture story seems to indicate very little drama on her part, very little in the way of defense.

It seems as if she does nothing to defend herself, because, truth told, she has ended up right where she knows she belongs.

How often I am this woman! I bow low to kiss the dirt, sure that I have earned my fate, that I deserve to be right where I am, buried under my sin and bruised and broken open by the guilty verdict I cannot rebuff. And more often than not, the fists waiting to cast the stones that will do me in are a million better versions of myself that I have not been, jeering and scoffing and mocking me in my weakness. Yes, the most sanctimonious Pharisee I ever face is the perfect version of myself, who just loves to barge into the heart of the real me—weak, tempted, sinner that I am—and pronounce her judgments with surety: failure, guilty, dirty, tainted, worthless.

If I know one thing for sure about this life in Christ, it is this: every one of us will have our "caught in the act" moments. They may be more or less dramatic than the one the Word offers us in the story of the woman caught in adultery. For us, the physical consequence is likely not public execution. But the Word tells us that the wages of sin is always death. Sometimes I think that perhaps a physical end to the misery may be easier to face than the spiritual stoning I daily wreak on myself when I am forced finally to admit who I have truly been. The terror of seeing my faults and failures on display and being utterly vulnerable feels worse than any physical pain anyone could ever inflict on me.

Have you been here before? Have you also been in that place where you have no more explanations, no more excuses to offer, no case to make in defense of yourself—where your silent shame is your only offering? Have you bent low and paid homage to the spiritual death sentence proclaimed over you by your own sin? Have you licked the dust of guilt and lain still, waiting for shame to stone you to death? Have you sneaked a look at the gathering crowd of judgment and found yourself looking back into your own eyes?

Yes, we are the certain sinners who are quick to consent to our own death sentence because we believe it is what we deserve. Crouched and scorned, we lay defeated at the feet of Jesus and wait for him to agree with the raised fists of judgment, wait for him to grab a stone with his hand, unstained by sin, and beat us into the ground with his perfection. This is the death of sin, the darkness that casts us so low that we forget who Jesus is, that we believe him our enemy, that we are certain that redemption was a lie and this time he will not come to our rescue.

But then our Jesus bends over and meets us in the dirt and dust. He dips his finger into our disgrace, and in doing so he transforms it. He meets us there in our defeat and stands to defend us when we will not defend ourselves. He meets the gaze of the crowd hungry for our demise, and in his voice there is not accord, but compassion. There is not judgment, but mercy.

Have you ever wondered what the secret message he traced in the dust said? What passed in the drawing of his finger where only her lowered eyes could see? I think, in the first time he stoops, our Jesus writes "forgiveness" over our sinful hearts. He pulls the plug on our internal panic buttons, remits our death sentence, leans low, and whispers, "Exhale, love. You are forgiven. Guilty? Yes. Doomed? No. Just breathe. I am here."

I wonder if as he leaned close he saw the hint of something familiar in her feminine features. I wonder if there was something about the curve of her chin or the way her hair fell across her brow that reminded him of his Mother, the first woman from whom he had learned love in his human form—the perfect woman. I wonder if he bent low to see the potential in our sister, there in the dirt, that she could not see in herself. I wonder if he recognized something of the hope of womanhood still echoing there in her, waiting to be called out. Maybe it was a certain kind of hope in her own possibility that he traced there in the sand, a possibility he knew because he had grown up under the tutelage of his own Mother, womanhood's fullest realization. Did he see his Mother reflected back at him in the face of this beloved one bent so low just now? And what was it that he traced in the dirt for her to see?

What he traced in the dirt may not have even mattered as much as the fact that, given the choice of stepping in with the stone throwers, he instead bent low and touched the dirt with the dust breathers. First, he forgives. And then, he speaks the words that save—the words we don't deserve, the words we could never merit, the words that revoke our death sentence and proclaim in its place life, hope, and wild grace. "Let anyone among you who is without sin be the first to throw a stone at her" (John 8:7). Jesus is not a liar. He does not offer justification for us. He does not pretend our failures are not real. What a relief, right? Because once you've been ripped open and exposed, who wants to wear the weight of pretending again? Once the lie has been exchanged for the truth, and we know how tired we were of telling it, there is no going back. And our God-man knows just what our exposed and vulnerable hearts need. Yes, it is what it is. We have been caught in the act. We are certain sinners. And we are no different from anyone else.

No, Jesus doesn't deny the truth, but he shines the light on the whole truth, the whole, wide story of human brokenness. This truth goes beyond the narrow story we sometimes tell ourselves, in which we are the only ones who get it wrong, who mess it up, who are bowed low in the dirt and the darkness.

Jesus reminds us of a truth we need to hear spoken over and over again: while our accusers may be right about us, they are wrong about him. He is not a God who shouts accusations with a clenched fist, but a God who bends low and traces forgiveness into the dirt of our sin. He is a God who sees our humanity as a condition worth redeeming rather than a defect worth burying.

He is a God who sees the likeness of himself bowed low in shame and who wants nothing more than to stand her up and restore her to her proper purposes. So as the fists lower and the shouts silence, he stoops down to us once again and traces a new word over us. He writes "redeemed" over our guilty verdict.

The second act to forgiveness is redemption. This is the part where he tells us not only to exhale but to stand, look him in the eye, and begin again. Because we are more than saved, more than not dead; we are restored to life, to purpose, to hope. We are not only encouraged to try again, but we are ordered to: "And Jesus said, 'Neither do I condemn you. Go your way, and from now on do not sin again'" (John 8:11).

It's not marching orders for a perfectionist meltdown that Jesus offers here. It is restoration, the fullness of redemption. It is his lifting us from the dirt and saying, "Yes, you fell, but you will not live here forever, in the dust of your sin. You will rise. You will walk out into your life again. And you will live. You will not half-live with the half-hope of having squeaked your way out of this one because I was nice. You will live full and purposeful, and you will walk in hope and radiant beauty because you are more than forgiven; you are free. The salvation you lost has been returned to you, and you have a new life to spend and invest in a new way. And I have faith in you, love. I know you will do better this time around. Go. You've got this."

This is our Jesus. He is a forgiver, yes, but even more, he is Redeemer, restorer.

~ WHO DOES HE SAY YOU ARE? ~
AN INVITATION TO DELIVERANCE

There is no woman who does not know the fear of being caught in the act of sin, who has not needed to be lifted up out of the ashes by her Savior. This is his mission of mercy to us. Yet, we can still convince ourselves that we are the only ones who fail him in the way we do. We can know with our minds that he will always forgive us, always offer us new mercies and new grace, but our hearts can wonder if whatever we were caught in might just be enough to disqualify us from full restoration.

Whatever it is you were doing when you were caught in the act, if you choose to read the words he has written over you, you will know that these words are true. You are a certain sinner, but you are also fully forgiven, fully redeemed, and fully restored to life. You don't just get a do-over. You get a whole new life with a whole new well of grace to draw from. You get your purpose back. You get to "go your way," the way that was laid out for you in his plans and purposes when he knit you together and wove you to reflect a unique facet of his perfection.

Jesus doesn't hand you a free pass for this one instance and leave you kneeling shamefaced in the dirt, still cowering before the accusation of your own sin. No, friend. Jesus does nothing halfway. He is complete in his love for you, complete in his mercy, complete in his promise to give you a new life. He restores your dignity, your worth, and your identity by raising you from the dust and standing you up again. And he sends you out to live again, assuring you that although you are a certain sinner you can at once be she who sinned and she who will sin no more. You are free. Grace has not only saved you but has restored you to your true purpose. You can go your way, living to love and serve the one who traced redemption in the dirt of your guilt and left the accusations, which said you could never be anything more, drooping in slack fists.

I think of the way the sacrament of confession works on my own soul, how often I start out afraid to confront my own sin and bring it into the light, forgetting that the goal is not for me to sit shamefaced with my sin but to draw it out so that my own healing can take place. I leave confession, not bowed lower because of facing my sin, but restored by God's mercy and sent out to live my purpose once again, to serve him with joy and hope. Jesus does not ignore my sin. He looks at it with the tenderness of his mercy and draws me up from it so that I may rise in freedom. You too, friend, can rise. Run to him, confess your sin, and let him lift you out of the ashes and restore you.

There is a deep fountain of grace waiting for you in Jesus. There is the grace you need to truly "go and sin no more"—a treasure of restoration—waiting for you on the other side of your confession. It is the reconciliation of your heart to his that restores you to your true purpose and transforms you into the woman he made you to be. On your own, you will quickly return to the dirt of your sin, but with his grace, you can walk in purpose again, restored and filled with the grace you need to live free from sin and its consequences. You can rise on the rich treasury of grace that awaits you in the sacrament and in the person of Christ.

Will you rise with me? Will you look around and see your freedom, your safety, in him? Will you believe him when he says that you can go and sin no more? Will you be the one who is not only forgiven but redeemed and restored? Will you be not only not dead but fully alive in him? This is his unbelievably generous gift to you and to me. Let us take hold of it and begin again. Let us go our way and earnestly strive to sin no more.

~ LET US PRAY ~

Jesus, my Redeemer and rescuer, sometimes I am not even sure what to say to you. I look up at you and see you reaching down to rescue me once again, and I want to turn away, to hide my tear-stained cheeks from your merciful gaze. Sometimes, it is all just too much, the way you love me when I know I don't deserve it.

I long for the day when I am not the sinner facedown in the dirt. I long for the day when I can approach you free and clean and pure. I wish I was more of what you call me to be. I sometimes wonder if the day will come when you won't reach down and trace forgiveness in the ashes of my brokenness, when you'll just walk away and let the world hurl its stones at me.

But you are more than a forgiver, Lord; you are a Redeemer. You not only lean down into the dirt to tell me that I have been given a forgiveness I do not deserve, but you take my hand and lift me up, and you believe in me. You believe I *can* "go and sin no more." You restore me to grace and purpose and dignity with your merciful touch. No matter how openly my sin has been exposed, no matter how certain my guilt, I can walk again. I can live a life of restored purpose and dignity because you are my Redeemer, and you do more than just forgive.

You reach into my dirt, not once, but twice—forgiving, and then giving me back what I have lost, lifting me up and sending me back into my life with your grace written over me.

Thank you, Lord. Give me the grace to face my sin, to be honest about my guilt, and then to see your hand reach down into my ashes, lift me up, and restore me to strength, to purpose, to dignity. Let me believe that no one is left to condemn me and that I am free to sin no more. Amen.

~ QUESTIONS FOR REFLECTION ~

1. What is leaving me feeling "caught in the very act" right now in my life? In what ways do I feel exposed and vulnerable because of my own faults and failings?

2. When was the last time I went to confession? How did it feel when I left? Is it time to go back?

3. Is there an area of my life about which I condemn myself, refusing to accept God's forgiveness, and believing that I am worthy of a spiritual death sentence?

4. If Jesus bent near to me right now and wanted to assure me of his forgiveness, what word might he trace in the dirt for me to see?

5. What do I need to do to be restored to full life again? What would it look like for me to "go and sin no more" and to live free from condemnation and restored to my true worth and purpose in Christ?

CHAPTER SEVEN

"YOU ARE MADE FOR CONTENTMENT"

Martha and Mary of Bethany

Now as they went on their way, [Jesus] entered a certain village, where a woman named Martha welcomed him into her home. She had a sister named Mary, who sat at the Lord's feet and listened to what he was saying. But Martha was distracted by her many tasks; so she came to him and asked, "Lord, do you not care that my sister has left me to do all the work by myself? Tell her then to help me." But the Lord answered her, "Martha, Martha, you are worried and distracted by many things; there is need of only one thing. Mary has chosen the better part, which will not be taken away from her."

—LUKE 10:38–42

· · · · ·

W hen Martha heard that Jesus was coming, she went and met him, while Mary stayed at home. Martha said to Jesus, "Lord, if you had been here, my brother would not have died. But even now I know that God will give you whatever you ask of him." Jesus said to her, "Your brother will rise again." Martha said to him, "I know that he will rise again in the resurrection on the last day." Jesus said to her, "I am the resurrection and the life. Those who believe in me, even though they die, will live, and everyone who lives and believes in me will never die. Do you believe this?" She said to him, "Yes, Lord, I believe that you are the Messiah, the Son of God, the one coming into the world."

—JOHN 11:20–27

. . . . .

Because I am a lot like Martha, I've always balked at the interpretations of this story that make it seem as if there is something intrinsically flawed in Martha's nature, or something intrinsically superior in her sister's. I've tried before to embrace the mindset that no matter how much my instincts tell me to get to the kitchen and get the supper ready, I should force myself to sit still at the Lord's feet all the time, to claim the better portion, to do the one thing that is necessary.

But do you know what happens every single time? My brain screams, "Food! Food is necessary. Someone has to do the work!" I end up just like Martha did in this story, agitated and resentful, feeling as if Jesus is playing favorites and I am automatically on the losing end because of the way he chose to make me. And that seems unjust.

But the more I look at this story and Jesus's words to Martha here, the more I am sure that Jesus never meant us to live in a world where we have to make a choice to be either a Martha or a Mary—where in order to seek holiness, we would have to change the temperament God gave us. I don't think our Jesus requires us to be something we are not in order to meet his approval.

Jesus was offering Martha, who was stuck in her either-or mindset, another option, the "both-and" option. He was extending to her an invitation to the one necessary thing, the one thing we need to live in intimacy with him, no matter how we are wired. He was extending to her in that moment, just as he extends to us now, an invitation to contentment, to live unhurried and unafraid, knowing that he is present, right here in the chaos of our everyday lives. And we can embrace that contentment whether we are natural sitters or natural servers. He is an equal-access Savior.

The truth is that any one of us could choose to sit at Jesus's feet and still be anxious and worried, distracted, missing out on the grace of the Savior's presence—just as we could also be in the kitchen contentedly laying supper out on a platter, while we tuned into Jesus's presence right there in our midst and drank of all that he had to offer.

What Jesus wants for you and me has very little to do with whether we sit or stand, serve the supper or contemplate at his feet. What he wants for us is to be so keenly aware of his divine presence with us that whatever we do takes on the nature of the extraordinary, and we live in a sense of wild gratitude. We can live knowing that we are completely surrounded by God, knowing that we are not working for his approval but for his pleasure. We can know that we are able to be utterly and completely confident and content in who we are and how we are wired because he is here, visiting us with his love and grace.

What great news, right? Jesus isn't asking you to fit into a box that feels constricting and ill-fitting so that he can call you good and holy. That's not the one thing that is necessary. Can you hear me exhaling with you?

What Jesus desires for us, more than he demands it from us, is for us to know that we belong to him. Whether we are the ones who by nature seek the spot at his feet, or the ones who tie up their apron strings and keep their hands busy, we can all be alert and attentive. We are all invited to be disciples.

And maybe, when we learn to be content in our own natural leanings, in the cellular makeup of our skin, maybe a wider spectrum of being will open up. Maybe suddenly we'll stop wiping those dishes dry and just leave them there sopping wet while we draw near to Jesus. Or maybe we'll stay, but the wiping will slow, the heavy sighs will silence, and our ears will tune in to the Master's voice instead of our own to-do list.

Jesus isn't looking for a world full of Marys, friend, any more than he is looking for a world full of Marthas. He is looking for a world full of women who know who they are and who it is they are called to serve, women who are content because they know he doesn't play favorites. He longs for women who know that he is universally accessible to each and every one of us, that he desires that we choose him over anxiety and worry, and that he longs for the contentment of our hearts.

Jesus longs for a world of women, of sisters, who will sit together at his feet and work together in his service, not looking to choose the better portion in order to be right or better or holier than one another, but to know Jesus more, love Jesus better, know Jesus more intimately, so that we can all stand or sit shoulder to shoulder and be content with who we are, how we are made, and what his unique calling is for our lives.

What if Martha had stood chopping things in her kitchen and let the knife slow and then stop while she took in fully what Jesus had to offer in that moment? What if she had paused to breathe a prayer of gratitude, so that the sound escaping from her lips in that moment of pause had been a contented sigh rather than agitation? What if she had then turned back to her chopping and preparing, filled with grace and with the presence of Jesus?

This is what Jesus desires to invite us into: a contentment that is not dependent on who we are but on who he is. Contentment is a theme throughout the Bible (see Proverbs 21:19; Ecclesiastes 5:1; Sirach 26:4). St. Paul professed, "I have learned to be content with whatever I have" (Philippians 4:11). Like him, we are called to be satisfied knowing that God is near, that he is trustworthy and good.

This is our calling as sisters in Christ. But isn't it so easy to lose sight of our own contentment, when it seems that some sister or another of ours may have outdone us in the race to land at Jesus's feet, may have out-jockeyed us for prime position? It can be difficult when we have been busy doing our work well, engaged in our given tasks, hoping they are forming our spirits in holiness, and we finally look up only to see that some other sister is even closer than we are, right up to his feet, sitting gloriously near while we stand seemingly too far away. We don't mean to let discontentment take root in our hearts, but it creeps in when we take our eyes off Jesus and put them on what everyone else is doing and where they are sitting, how they are serving, and how it always seems that so many others are so much closer to Jesus than we are.

When Jesus turns to Martha and says, "Martha, Martha, you are worried and distracted about many things," he is inviting her not to worry—not to worry about position or place or who is better than who. He is inviting her not to worry about what her sister is doing or where she is sitting. None of that matters. Only one thing matters. And it is not whether Martha is more likely to sit still and listen or to fidget in the kitchen. It is that he, the Master, is completely available and accessible to each one of us, with our unique makeups and temperaments, and he desires us to be content in his presence, to be satisfied, to know that he is completely ours and we are completely his, just as are each of our sisters in Christ.

Jesus loves Martha as much as he loves Mary. Jesus longs for friendship with Martha as much as he longs for friendship with Mary. He is not out to make Martha feel badly about herself, but he wants to invite her to think wider, deeper, beyond the place where she stands, toward the state of her heart. Jesus wasn't angry or frustrated with Martha when she missed the point that day. He was saddened. She was missing out on the very thing that he had come to offer her, and the one thing he wanted her to have: contentment.

Mary's better portion was not that she was the quieter, more contemplative sister. Mary's better portion, in that moment, was that her eyes were off Martha and on Jesus. Mary's better portion was not dependent on her natural inclinations or on whether she ended up physically closer to Jesus than Martha. The better portion she chose was to set aside the worry and anxiety that comes from measuring our worth by comparing ourselves to those around us, and to instead gaze fully on the face of her Savior who was there with her, present to her and offering her a freely given, unearned stamp of approval out of love. Leaning in, she wasn't worried about what she could offer him, but she focused on what she could learn from him.

CONTENTMENT EVEN IN GRIEF

Later, when Jesus returns to Bethany after he learns of Lazarus's death, as we read in the Gospel of John, we see that Martha and Mary have embraced this lesson fully. This time it is Martha who arrives first at the feet of Jesus, who testifies to her faith in him. Then she runs back and calls Mary, and both sisters end up in the same place. Both become some of the first witnesses to the hope of resurrection. Jesus is drawn to their confident faith, and he weeps for his friend Lazarus and for their tears.

Martha is courageous in her pleading and in her testimony of faith this time. She is confident in who she is in Jesus, ever the one to come out to welcome, to think of the details, to fuss over proprieties. But now she is also sure that Jesus is there for her. She finds comfort in his presence and has the courage to ask him for what her heart most longs for. She knows her place is secure with Jesus; she has learned to be content with his will and to have faith in his love for her.

Mary runs out behind her, sure of her place at Jesus's feet, and she echoes Martha's courageous faith. It is that faith that invites the miracle of Lazarus's return from the dead. It is the faith of Martha and Mary that gets a first glimpse of life beyond death, of resurrection joy.

This is the desire of his heart for us, friends. He doesn't ask that we compete for holiness or that we mold ourselves into some ill-fitting definition in order to appease him. But he wants us to learn to accept the grace of being loved by him, to learn to be content in who we are in him, so that we can be confident of what he can do for us. That contentment grows naturally into deep friendship with him, and deep friendship with him gives us a courageous faith that runs to him with all our needs and all our hopes and all our sorrows. We all end up at just the same place, dear sisters: close to him, where there is room for all of us and where he is waiting to reveal his goodness and his glory to us. There is no position that pleases Jesus more than the one that reveals the disposition of a heart that knows her place with him is secure.

I am guessing that when we can embrace that good truth, sister, we will soon find that there is room at his feet for all of us, and that even those of us who are most like Martha will want to take their place, and sit at the feet of the Savior, shoulder to shoulder with their sisters, content in his presence. What joy there is waiting there for us! Let us take our places, friend, content to be who we are in his presence.

~ WHO DOES HE SAY YOU ARE? ~

AN INVITATION TO CONTENTMENT

Worry and anxiety are born when we let Jesus's presence with us and longing for friendship with us be eclipsed by our concerns over what we need to be doing to please him. They fester and grow when we become preoccupied with what everyone else is doing that seems to earn more of his attention, more of his approval, that appears to bring them closer to him and to give them an advantage over us.

How easily I am tricked into believing that the key to holiness is doing *more* for Jesus, rather than being who I can *be* in Jesus. Over and over again I find myself wiping the sweat from my brow as agitation creeps into my throat. *It's not fair, Lord. Make someone else work as hard as I am.* Sometimes I fail to consider that perhaps what Jesus desires from me is not just another pair of hands. Instead, what he wants is something truly liberating for me: contentment.

This contentment is the freedom Jesus invites us to experience in this show of love to the sisters at Bethany. We do not have to find a way to be something we are not in order to please Jesus. We do not have to work for his approval. We only have to keep our gaze on him, to lean in and listen from whatever position we find ourselves, and to know that he is near. This is the only necessary thing for us to do to find contentment in our lives.

And, oh, how I long for contentment! How I long to be free of the pressures and the worries that drive my days, from striving for some picture-perfect version of womanhood I assume everyone else is easily achieving. I long to know that there is room for all of us with all our gifts and temperaments in the heart of our Savior, and to know that—more than he desires us to do or be any particular thing—he simply desires that we be satisfied in him.

If I could grab on to that truth and hold it tight as I go about my daily hustle and bustle, how different would my heart look at the end of the day? If I could live free of the pressures of comparing and striving, and instead know that I have full access to Jesus just as I am, just where I am right now in my life, how much more would I be able to hear his voice and respond?

And if I was absolutely sure that I was approved of, welcomed, and invited into full friendship with Jesus, along with every other sister on the big, wide earth, how differently would I feel about the women in my life? How much more fully would I celebrate what it means to be sisters in Christ? Contentment frees us to receive with grateful hearts the love and affirmation Jesus comes to offer us, and to offer that same love and affirmation to one another, because all our reasons for fearing one another are melted away in the light of Christ.

This is Jesus's invitation to Martha, to Mary, and to each of us. We can live a life of contentment, fully satisfied with who we are and how we are loved, free of comparison, because of Jesus. In him, we have all we need to be full and to be free, whatever our unique needs, longings, desires, or temperaments are. This is what he offers us when he comes to visit us, to dwell with us, to be present to us: an intimacy with him that fills us so completely that we have no need to long for anything more. This is the better portion, the one thing necessary. And he offers it to each of us, just as we are, freely and without reserve. He doesn't just offer it, but he longs for us to receive it, and he desires for us to feel it.

Martha was missing this better portion, not because she was more of a doer than a listener, not because she was more extroverted than introverted, not because she was more active than contemplative. No, she was missing it because she thought she had to earn it, that her worthiness was determined by how well she could serve the Lord. She was anxious and worried because, as she strove for his approval, she looked around and saw that someone had gotten there before her, and that seemed wrong because of all the effort she was putting forth.

Are you still striving, friend? Are you still running yourself ragged looking to have something to offer the Lord to make you worthy of him? Do you look around you and wonder how so many people seem to have gotten so much closer to him while you have been working so hard and still feel so far away?

Here's the good news for today, for you and me both. We can quit the striving and the working and the approval seeking. We can exhale and fill our lungs with the fresh air of acceptance, of appreciation, of being invited into full friendship with Christ. We can be content, satisfied, and grateful. And we don't have to do a thing to earn it, to deserve it. We don't need to jockey for position. All we have to do is look up and see him here, beckoning us nearer, and then choose to be drawn in by his loving gaze and tuned into his voice.

~ LET US PRAY ~

Master, today I acknowledge that I am free, free to be myself and to draw near to you. Thank you, Lord, that it is not my position that determines how close I am to you, but my disposition—that it matters less what my hands are doing and more what my heart is hearing.

Lord, free me from the lie that my sisters are better than me. Free me from the fear that I am somehow not made right for holiness. Free me from the agitation and irritation that plague my soul when those thoughts are louder than your voice.

You are my teacher and my friend. Help me know and embrace that. Help me live in the acceptance and approval you offer me without expectations. Help me, Lord, to be fully satisfied in knowing that you are near, always near enough for me to hear you teach me and lead me and guide me, if only I will listen. If my hands are busy serving you, still I can listen. And if you draw me near and make me sit quietly, still I can listen.

There is no first place in intimacy with you, Lord. There is only one necessary thing—the better portion—which is having a heart content in knowing that it is in the presence of God, who offers his approval freely.

Let me embrace contentment today, Teacher. Draw near to me, and let me know that you are God. And in that knowledge, let me long for nothing more. Amen.

~ QUESTIONS FOR REFLECTION ~

1. When I first heard the story of Mary and Martha, did I wish I was more like one or the other? Did one strike me as holier than the other? Why?

2. Do I have a tendency to compare myself to other women and see them as holier than me? How does this affect my relationship with Jesus?

3. What does it mean to me to be content? Am I experiencing contentment in my spiritual walk? What contributes to my contentment or discontentment?

4. What is one thing I could do every day, as I go about my daily life of service to those around me, to remind myself that the Lord is present with me and to still my heart to hear his voice?

CHAPTER EIGHT

"You Honor Christ"

The Sinful Woman Who Anoints Jesus

One of the Pharisees asked Jesus to eat with him, and he went into the Pharisee's house and took his place at the table. And a woman in the city, who was a sinner, having learned that he was eating in the Pharisee's house, brought an alabaster jar of ointment. She stood behind him at his feet, weeping, and began to bathe his feet with her tears and to dry them with her hair. Then she continued kissing his feet and anointing them with the ointment. Now when the Pharisee who had invited him saw it, he said to himself, "If this man were a prophet, he would have known who and what kind of woman this is who is touching him—that she is a sinner." Jesus spoke up and said to him, "Simon, I have something to say to you." "Teacher," he replied, "speak." "A certain creditor had two debtors; one owed five hundred denarii, and the other fifty. When they could not pay, he canceled the debts for both of them. Now which of them will love him more?" Simon answered, "I suppose the one for whom he canceled the greater debt." And Jesus said to him, "You have judged rightly." Then turning toward the woman, he said to Simon, "Do you see this woman? I entered your house; you gave me no water for my feet, but she has bathed my feet with her tears and dried them with her hair. You gave me no kiss, but from the time I came in she has not stopped kissing my feet. You did not anoint my head with oil, but she has anointed my feet with ointment. Therefore, I tell you, her sins, which were many, have been forgiven; hence she has shown great love. But the one to whom little is forgiven, loves little." Then he said to her, "Your sins are forgiven." But those who were at the table with him began to say among themselves, "Who is this who even forgives sins?" And he said to the woman, "Your faith has saved you; go in peace."

—LUKE 7:36–50

. . . . .

She did not have much to offer him, no tribute worthy of the Master. She was an outcast, while he had dined at the tables of the prominent, taught in the Temple, and called God his Father. She was a sinner, while he might be the Messiah. And, yet, as she watched him walk the dusty roads of her homeland, she saw something different in him, something surprising, something that compelled her to draw near.

She was a woman of the city and a sinner. I am quite certain that "sinner" is biblical code language for a particular sin, but, really, who of us can claim not to deserve the same title? I am a woman of the mission field—and a sinner. You might be a woman of the kitchen sink or the office desk—and a sinner. But in truth, we are all, like this woman, walking around with broken hearts and bruised spirits, with stained souls and painful burdens. We are the lowly and afflicted ones.

There have been moments in my life—especially in the early months and years of grieving the death of my son—where I felt like my identity was completely reduced to my broken heart. I was entirely consumed by sadness and grief. I was lonely and afraid. More than anything, I wanted to draw near to and be comforted by my Jesus in that pain. The very real man, the Jesus who reclines at tables as he visits with friends, the Jesus with dusty feet and dirt under his nails, the Jesus who is wholly, truly present to the ones who want to know him—this is the Jesus I needed.

And yet, that strong desire to lean in to the heart of my Savior was always shadowed by looming anxiety. I wondered if Jesus wanted me when all I had to offer was a broken heart. Could I honor the Son of Man if the only gift I brought to lay at his feet was my grief?

I wonder if this woman—this sinful woman, this woman of the city—was feeling that same confusion in her spirit the evening she made her way into a private dinner party, her eyes fixed on the Master, alabaster jar of ointment in her hand. As the lump in her throat grew into a painful ache and she blinked back the tears, was she wondering if her offering would be enough? Did she tremble as she tried to decide how much her broken heart was worth to the Messiah?

Perhaps that is why she approaches him from behind—longing to honor him, with only a simple jar of ointment and a desire to draw near to him and feel his humanity in her hands, yet also frightened, wondering if he will see her true intent. She takes her place "behind him" and "at his feet," maybe in a double desire to draw as close as possible to the human nature of her God and at the same time not assume that he will welcome her, giving him space to leave her in the dark and not turn his face to her.

How often I have been the woman at once drawn to the heart of my Savior and yet questioning my worth to him! I want to trust in his love for me, but I am afraid to approach with what seems so little to offer; I'm uncertain that my simple trust is enough to honor him. Have you been there too? Have you been desperate to get closer to the Lord but tentative and afraid that you don't have anything to offer that will honor him and earn your place at his feet?

Can I tell you a little secret about our sweet Jesus, friend? He does not have disposable disciples. He doesn't use us like paper plates at a party, tossing us out when we get messy. No, God values the hearts of his precious daughters like they are vessels of the highest quality, like the finest china. If we find ourselves messy, used up, chipped, and even totally broken in service to him, he will find a way to wash us clean, put us back together again, and put us on display as his prized possessions. We, friend, are worth far more to him than we could ever imagine.

And when we come to him in our brokenness and offer him our tears, our pain, the most intimate places of our own broken hearts, do you know what he says of us? He says that we have loved well, loved much. He forgives us our sins, accepts the beauty of our offering, and says it is our faith that has saved us. Jesus doesn't look at our brokenness and recoil from us. He looks at the trust and vulnerability with which we offer it, and he reaches for us, coming close to bring comfort and peace to our hurting hearts, even if we ourselves are the cause of our own brokenness.

This woman walked into the home of a Pharisee, a place where laws and rules and propriety reigned, and broke them all with her one weeping, broken heart. Desperate to bless her Lord and God, to honor him in some way, despite the sin and pain that had come to define her, she drew as near to him as humanly possible, beyond what was socially acceptable, in a confident intimacy that left the rule followers and acceptability enforcers uncomfortable, wondering what kind of prophet would allow such a thing.

She leaned in close enough for her tears to fall right onto his feet, then leaned closer still as she wiped them with her hair, and then at the peak of her defiant intimacy—a closeness inconsiderate of all social norms and proprieties—she kissed his human skin. She turned the world's rules on end and, perhaps for the first time in her life, leaned in not to the skin of a man but to the heart of a Savior who loved her with a kind of love she had never known.

She breaks her little alabaster jar of perfumed ointment over his feet, an act of humble service and recognition of his worthiness to be served. She doesn't just pour out a bit of what she has to offer; she breaks it wide open and pours it all out, everything she brought to honor him. Her offering is a sacrificial one, for the ointment is costly. Whether the woman has taken the ointment from her own home or purchased it just for this purpose, we know it is a sacrifice for her to offer it, and to offer it so fully. But she holds none of it back for herself. She pours out every bit of what she has in order to honor Jesus. And as she does, she feels his invitation to keep leaning in further to him.

Based on other Gospel accounts, some theologians have surmised that the woman who anoints Jesus could be Mary Magdalene or Mary of Bethany (see Dr. Marcellino D'Ambrosio's article "Saint Mary Magdalene" at CrossroadsInitiative.com). However, in this account, the woman remains unnamed, and we know only that she is considered a sinner. Whether these are different accounts of the same event or similarly themed accounts of different events, we can conclude that Jesus opened himself to this kind of familiarity with women, both with women he knew as friends and with women who simply drew near to him because of who he was.

We honor Christ when we are willing to draw near and sit with him in that tension, in the place where the pain of the passion and the joy of the resurrection meet for our salvation. When we pour ourselves out fully and offer our anointing, in the midst of both suffering and hope, opening ourselves to the full spectrum of what it means to encounter Christ, he is honored. All he desires is that we hold nothing back of what we have to offer. He asks that—like our sister here, be she Mary Magdalene or Mary of Bethany or simply a woman who knows she is a sinner—we pour out all we have and trust that it honors him.

It is as if, each time she leaned closer to Jesus, his love called her deeper into his pure heart, a heart that loved her freely and without self-interest. So she was able to lean in beyond her heartbreak, beyond the expectations of the world around her, past the boundaries of convention and her own sinful status, and straight into the heart of the Savior. And there, in the intimate depths of her soul, she loved him well.

~ WHO DOES HE SAY YOU ARE? ~
AN INVITATION TO INTIMACY

Are you ready to risk that kind of love with your Jesus? Are you ready to love deeper than your doubts about your own worth, deeper than your heartache, deeper than the expectations of onlookers and the rule books of a stingy, false faith would ever allow? Are you ready to believe that your desire to love him is enough for Jesus, that he is honored by the pouring out of your heart and the drawing in of your soul?

This is the truth, friend. We are saved by the faith that draws us near enough that he can touch us. We are saved by a desire to love him well. We are saved when the tears of our brokenness touch his perfection. We are saved when we step across the lines of convention and safe distances to kiss the skin of our God. We are saved when we offer him the kind of love that breaks itself open and pours itself out in a holy anointing of faith mingled with our broken humanity. We are saved when we carry the ointment of our worship in a tiny alabaster jar and mingle it with the salt of our tears and swishing of our hair right over our Savior's dust-laden feet.

This is the faith that saves us. This is the kind of love that honors Christ.

What is the heartbreak that leaks out in your tears, and what sacred gift do you hold in your alabaster jar? How deep will you lean in to Jesus to make them a holy offering of love to him? What if you risked going all the way? What if you offered him all the tears and pain, leaning all the way in to him, pouring out all the goodness you carry in your alabaster heart? You give him honor when you give him all.

What if you believed that the ointment of your life, poured out freely and without reserve, could both ease the suffering of Christ's passion and celebrate the joy of his resurrection? If you can sit in the glorious tension of that, drawing deeper into the mystery of what it means to love him well, then you can trust that he will open his heart to you and receive your offering of self as gift, a gift that honors him, Messiah and friend of sinners.

Maybe you've felt the creeping doubt that your sin is too much, or that what you do for him is not enough. Maybe you have been your own worse Pharisee, telling yourself that if he only knew what kind of woman you truly were, he would never let you draw near to him. Maybe you've applied his unusual kingdom economy to others, but forgotten that it is for you too: the system where the greater your debt is and the greater liability you have been, the more worth you have to the Master.

Here's the thing we all have to believe: Jesus cares so much less than we do about what we have done against him and what we can do for him. His eyes are trained on our bending down, leaning in, and pouring out. He has tunnel vision for love and mercy. If we offer ourselves to him in love and receive his mercy freely, we will become his greatest assets—they who have loved much.

This story of the woman who bows and bends to her Jesus, who pours out her burden in her tears and her blessings from a broken vial, who kisses his feet in an act of fully surrendered love—this can be our story too. We can be the woman who ignores the watchers and the waiters who are looking for our moment of rebuke, the woman who draws near to Jesus and embraces him with a desire to love him well. We can be women who honor Christ because we love him with a risky, intimate love that longs simply to be close enough to touch our lips to his divinity.

We can be the women who taste and see the goodness of the Lord, in our sin, in our heartbreak, in our brokenness. We can be the women who use what they have to honor Christ and trust that it is enough.

We can be the bowers and the benders to his glory, the weepers with repentant hearts, the humble ones who pour our offerings out of broken vials, the lovers who seal our drawing in with a kiss. We can be these women because he invites us to be so. He reclines and waits for us, knows when we are there in the shadows, and beckons us in, even if we come hesitantly from behind.

And he is honored when we lean in to love him well. This is the faith that saves us. This is the faith that sets us free. This is the way we honor Christ the King.

~ LET US PRAY ~

Jesus, Master and friend, here I am, longing to be close to you. I long to draw near and know you deeply, intimately. Is it okay to need you this much? Is it all right that I desire to touch and feel and hold you in my hands so I can be assured that all your goodness, all your holiness, and all your love for me are real? Of course it is. Because you are my Jesus, and this is your way. You wait patiently for me to draw near to you, you encourage me, you remove the obstacles from my path, and then you minister to me as I come close to you.

I wish I had more to offer, Lord—more than the same old tears and sin and broken heart, more than a tiny vial full of fragrant love, more than myself and all my broken mess poured out to you. But this is me, Jesus. And this is all I have.

Thank you for seeing the gift of me, for holding my offering with tenderness and intimacy, for never making me feel ashamed, alone, or rejected when I find the courage to lean in close to you.

Give me the courage today to draw nearer still. Help me to know that there is an endless ocean of love and friendship with you for me to discover. Remind me that I can always lean further, pour out more, love you more deeply. Give me the desire to do so, good Master.

I am here, bowing low and leaning close, Jesus. I am offering myself to you. Lean in and let me know that I am loved. Amen.

~ QUESTIONS FOR REFLECTION ~

1. In what ways do I draw near to Jesus? How do I seek closeness with him?
2. What are the obstacles that keep me from growing into a deeper intimacy with the Lord? What fears keep me at a distance from him?

3. Do I ever feel inhibited from offering myself to Jesus just as I am? Am I willing to embarrass myself, for Jesus's sake?

4. What is in my alabaster jar? What do I have, even in the smallest portion, that can be a fragrant offering to Jesus, a gift to honor him?

CHAPTER NINE

"You Can Stand Tall"

The Woman Crippled by a Demon

Now he was teaching in one of the synagogues on the sabbath. And just then there appeared a woman with a spirit that had crippled her for eighteen years. She was bent over and was quite unable to stand up straight. When Jesus saw her, he called her over and said, "Woman, you are set free from your ailment." When he laid his hands on her, immediately she stood up straight and began praising God. But the leader of the synagogue, indignant because Jesus had cured on the sabbath, kept saying to the crowd, "There are six days on which work ought to be done; come on those days and be cured, and not on the sabbath day." But the Lord answered him and said, "You hypocrites! Does not each of you on the sabbath untie his ox or his donkey from the manger, and lead it away to give it water? And ought not this woman, a daughter of Abraham whom Satan bound for eighteen long years, be set free from this bondage on the sabbath day?" When he said this, all his opponents were put to shame; and the entire crowd was rejoicing at all the wonderful things that he was doing.

—LUKE 13:10–17

. . . . .

She doesn't seem the most likely candidate for a miracle. She isn't bleeding out her lifeblood or on the verge of being stoned to death. She's simply bent over, unable to stand up straight. She is bent over by a demon, Scripture says. But this story also bears little resemblance to the other stories of demonic possession we see in the Gospels. There are no flailing limbs and foaming mouths, no growls and grunts, none of the drama we remember and fear.

It's a quiet scene, really. There is Jesus teaching in the synagogue, the way that rabbis do. A woman makes her way into the picture. She "appears just then," the story tells us, as if she just happens to walk by at the moment Jesus is there, not accidentally, but in a moment of divine intervention.

Still, she doesn't approach him, fall at his feet, and beg for healing. She doesn't call out to him or even reach desperately for the hem of his cloak. She simply makes her way into the synagogue, hunched, crippled, unable to stand straight.

But Jesus knows there is something more to her story. He is immediately drawn to her and calls her over to him. I wonder if the awareness of the Evil One shudders through him, if he senses it deep in his bones. Because he does not just let this woman pass by and stay stooped and bent low. No, he has sensed what is happening here, and he is not going to let Satan get away with her.

I wonder too about this woman's disability. She is bent, stooped over. How did that happen? Did she just bend all at once? Was she overcome by this evil spirit in one single blow? Or was it gradual disabling? Did Satan begin a slow whisper over her that bent her lower and lower over the years as she gave in to believing him? How long did it take for her to be crippled by his evil ways, to no longer be able to stand tall?

I wonder because I know that I am susceptible to the same evil spirit; her disability has often been my own. I know how often I have been dis-abled by Satan's whispered lies, how often I have bent my head and shuffled my feet after the first whispers of his deceit, and soon found myself stooping low beneath the burden of lies he has heaped on my back.

Backbones are the things of courage. The world tells us to grow one, get one, use ours to stand tall and stand up for ourselves. If only it were that easy. But how often do we find ourselves bending under the weight of the world's mixed messages, which tell us at once to pull ourselves up and puff ourselves out with a false sense of self-worth, and at the same time constantly yell at us that every effort is not good enough?

The lies start there, as we bend our spirit to the world's relentless demands, to the dizzying spin of its commands to do this and be that. And then Satan, opportunist that he is, takes advantage of our momentary weakness by barging into our spirits and magnifying the lies the world has told us. He is the master spinner of deceit, the great finger-pointing accuser who can transform our doubts and insecurities into bondage and oppression while disguising his voice as the sweetness of the Spirit of God.

I wish I could pretend it was hard for me to relate to this woman, brought so low by Satan that she has been crippled, disabled. But I am all too familiar with a back that bends under the weight of his lies.

The weight of my very real failures weakens my backbone; my self-confidence lags in the wake of the ways I get it all wrong every day. Mothering, marriage, friendship with others and with Christ, virtue, humility, holiness—they all elude me regularly enough that my courage slumps and my posture slacks.

And then, almost imperceptibly, Satan sneaks in with his lies. Suddenly my momentary failures are monumental character flaws, and I am surrounded by the surety that I am an unredeemable, doomed disappointment. I will never be a good enough mother, no matter how hard I try. I will never treat my husband as well as he deserves to be treated. I will never be kind enough or generous enough or thoughtful enough to the people who love me. I will never be humble enough or holy enough to be pleasing to anyone. I will never be good enough for God.

It's strange how we can see those things in stark print and know for certain they are not true, yet somehow Satan is able to bind them into a bundle so convincing that we willingly let him lay it across our backs and bend us low. His lies are so silly when we see them in clarity, but the King of Lies is skillful and knows just how to sweeten his speech so it whispers confusion and disappointment long enough that they become crippling to our spirits.

I don't know what the lies are that Satan uses to bend you. I don't know what he tries to lay across your back like an unbearable burden so that you are unable to straighten yourself. But I do know why he does it. I know why he did it to the woman in this story, and I know why he continues to do it to women today, to us.

Being in the presence of an evil spirit for eighteen years had crippled this woman. And that is what Satan hopes to do to us as well. He wants to disable us—to rob us of our God-given identity, ability, gifts, and purposes until we are unable to stand tall in Christ.

When we as women are bent and bowed low, crippled by the false burdens of self-doubt and self-loathing, disabled from living our true purposes, evil has an open door to do its work, and half the army of the redeemed is unable to stand at attention and fight the good fight. Perhaps this is the why behind the unlikely miracle in this story. Jesus does not take the disabling of a woman by Satan's lies lightly. There is no warrior woman that he will let fall into enemy hands as if she were just another casualty of the inevitable battle between the kingdoms of light and darkness.

No, friend, you and I are invaluable to him. He will not have us bent low and unable to stand tall. There is no lie of Satan that he lets pass as acceptable when it comes to the daughters of his Father.

I wonder if the certain bend, the slant of the head, the lowering of the eyes, the stooping of the shoulders in just that way, is unique—if Jesus recognizes it right upon seeing it. I wonder if something in his divinity shudders and rises to anger the moment he sees her approaching. I wonder what the spiritual battle for this daughter of the King, which we do not see in the story, looked like. Did fire flash in Jesus's eyes and the spirit run from fear straightaway? Did Jesus feel the power go out of him before he even saw her? Or did the enemy creep quietly away the moment he sensed the presence of the Lord? We will never know. But what we do know is this: her freedom was not won easily—it never is—but it mattered to Jesus that she be set free.

It matters so much that he doesn't even wait for her to approach him, reach him, or call out for him. He calls to her straightaway, calls freedom out to her—the voice of God claiming her as his own and setting her free from Satan's snare.

Jesus knows how we are made. He knows what our hearts need to believe, what our deepest longing truly is. So he steps toward her and touches her, laying his hands on her. When you have lived stooped and bent by what Satan says about you for eighteen long years, when he has whispered deceit and thievery into your spirit for so long, you need the power of God to save you, but you also need the love of God to heal you, to remind you who you are. You need him to come close and hold your hand while you remember how to stand tall again.

I can almost feel the physical relief in her body, the great wash of relief in her limbs as her spine straightens. I feel it in my own bones, the pulling straight of each vertebra as the Lord touches all the spots that I have allowed to stoop over with the weight of the lies Satan has told me. I feel myself thinking of my Jesus looking at me with compassionate eyes and calling freedom out to me, "You are enough. You are good. You are faithful. You are lovely. You are a delight to my heart. You are mine." Like gears clicking back into place, my spine straightens as my soul feels the strength of its freedom. I stand tall again, as the burden of lies I took up without even realizing I was doing it falls away.

~ WHO DOES HE SAY YOU ARE? ~
AN INVITATION TO "COME AWAY"

Sometimes I get so engaged in my life of missionary service, so busy in the doing, that I do not even realize how stooped I have become, how weary I really am. Then a moment comes that makes it so clear to me that it feels as if I might never be able to take another step forward.

Recently, I had the opportunity to take the trip of a lifetime with my husband and almost backed my way out of it because I was bent so low by all my doing that I began to believe that I did not deserve rest, did not merit that kind of blessing. It was a certain lie, easily detectable as I type it now. But these lies are sinewy and sly when fatigue fogs your heart and Satan can come in easily cloaked by your own exhaustion.

One night as I lie considering if the tickle in my throat might just be the beginning of an illness strong enough to buy me a pass to stay home, curled up and cuddling my burdens and Satan's lies like treasures, the Lord extended me an invitation as I journaled. The words came thus, "Come away with me, please. And delight in me the way that I delight in you." "Delight" is a word that we so often take to mean something silly, whimsical, wholly unnecessary. Yet, this is the word that Scripture uses over and over again to tell us how God responds to the existence of us, his daughters.

There was a gentle truth in that invitation that dispelled the false burden that had bent me low with weariness. I began to straighten, to listen again to the voice of the Lover of my soul rather than the Prince of Lies. And do you know, on that trip not only did I find joy and delight in the Lord and the detailed ways that he loved and wooed me, but I found rest, renewal, and restoration—the very things that I thought I needed to grab for myself rather than accept what God was offering. Jesus was calling me close to him so he could unbind my burdens and straighten me to standing again. And I almost missed it.

Are you feeling it too, friend? Can you hear Jesus calling out to you, setting you free, releasing you from the burdens you carry, and giving you strength to stand tall again? And then do you feel his drawing near, the weight of his hands on your shoulders, his steady gaze drawing your head and neck up for the first time in ages? Close your eyes for a just a moment and feel it. Here and now, freedom is washing over you, your backbone of courage is growing strong once again, your head is lifted with grace. Feel yourself grow tall with confidence because you have been set free.

Every lie that Satan has told you about who you are has been blasted away by love. The truth has been spoken over you. The weight of false identity that you have carried, the spirit that has whispered the falsehoods in your ears—they are all gone when Christ is near. He calls you free, and you are free indeed. He puts his hands on you, and you are fully yourself again, standing tall in him.

He cares not what Satan says nor what the Pharisees of the world say. He cares not what lies you have been told or what the rules might be that say you should stay bound one day more. Every obstacle to your freedom is nothing in his presence, and every reason the world could give him for leaving you bound is unacceptable in his eyes. He sees your stoop, friend, and he runs to you, sending his divine grace before him, and you are free before you even realize how near he has drawn.

His voice is calling out across the veil to you today. It is calling out freedom, courage, strength. His hands are reaching out to touch you; they are lifting your chin to meet his gaze, lifting your head to face the world with confidence, and straightening your backbone so you can stand tall.

He does all this because you are his, and no enemy shall prevail against you. He who is Truth is setting you free, and you shall be free indeed. And in that freedom, you can stand tall. And so can I. Let us stand together, you and I, courageous in our true identity and done with the lies that Satan has whispered for far too long. Let us learn to look at one another with Jesus's eyes, to recognize the bent and the slight slope of the neck when the enemy creeps back in; and over and over as many times as it takes, let us call freedom over one another, we fellow daughters of God, sisters in Christ.

Let us be an army of soldiers whose freedom the enemy fears, who stay strong because we believe the truth the Lord has spoken over us, and we repeat the call to one another so that we all remain standing tall.

~ LET US PRAY ~

O, sweet Jesus, in you is truth and freedom. And, oh, how I need them both. This enemy of ours, Lord, is a wily and wicked foe. I know his game. I know how he creeps and crawls and makes his way in with his lies. And yet, over and over again, he gets to me. It is so easy to convince me that I am not who you say that I am. Too quickly, I bend and bow to his deceptions; too readily I accept his burden of negativity: not enough, failure, never good, unwanted, unacceptable, unloved.

And my backbone weakens, Lord. The courage I need to stand up to his lies and stand tall in you slacks. I need you to call to me, to remind me, Jesus, of my freedom. I need you to fight this battle on my behalf. And I need you to reach out to me, take hold of my heart, and remind me who it is you say that I am.

Jesus, I want to lay down this burden that bends and bows me low. I want to stand tall in the identity you have given me. I want to lift my head in confident freedom because you have called it out over me. Draw near, Lord, and remind me again. I am so sorry that I let the Evil One whisper to me over and over again, that I give him my strength. But I am grateful that you always see me, recognize the stoop in my shoulders, and won't let me stay bound to his false burdens.

I lift my eyes to you, Lord. I will keep them raised to your holy face. Give me strength to stand tall when the enemy creeps in again. Give me grace to walk in the truth of who I am in you. And, Jesus, make me like you—able to see my sisters and the way they have been crippled by his lies too. Give me a generous, compassionate heart that calls freedom out over them in the way you have done for me. Give me courage, Lord, so that I can give the same to your daughters who need it. Amen.

~ QUESTIONS FOR REFLECTION ~

1. What are the lies Satan whispers to me to burden my heart and discourage me?

2. How can I recognize when the Evil One has been at work in my spirit? How does he cripple me?

3. What would it look like for me to walk in freedom from those lies, to embrace my abilities and the identity I have in Christ?

4. How can I help other women let go of the lies by which they have been stooped low and help them stand tall in Christ again?

CHAPTER TEN

"You Can Pray Boldly"

The Syrophoenician Woman

From there [Jesus] set out and went away to the region of Tyre. He entered a house and did not want anyone to know he was there. Yet he could not escape notice, but a woman whose little daughter had an unclean spirit immediately heard about him, and she came and bowed down at his feet. Now the woman was a Gentile, of Syrophoenician origin. She begged him to cast the demon out of her daughter. He said to her, "Let the children be fed first, for it is not fair to take the children's food and throw it to the dogs." But she answered him, "Sir, even the dogs under the table eat the children's crumbs." Then he said to her, "For saying that, you may go—the demon has left your daughter." So she went home, found the child lying on the bed, and the demon gone.

—MARK 7:24–30

. . . . .

When my children were young, I developed a terrible habit: I never served myself a plate during breakfast and lunch. I would simply scrounge the leftovers from their half-eaten meals as I ran from serving to picking up to washing the dishes and back to caring for and training up their little bodies and souls. I began to live as though I was not worthy of anything more than scraps, not only of food, but even of grace. I acted as if only I tried harder, dug deeper, and got it right more often, I would be holy enough to ask Jesus for more help—but not now. *As I am now*, I thought, *I am not worthy to ask for more of him.*

The Syrophoenician woman in this reading comes to us with an interesting set of descriptors. The single word by which she is named, Syrophoenician, defines her as an outsider, unworthy even to be in the presence of good Jewish men, much less one known as a rabbi. She is a Gentile, one not even worthy of a nod of acknowledgment, much less to be granted a miracle of grace by the Savior of the Jews.

In addition to her cultural status as an outsider, this woman has a daughter who is possessed by demons. I do not know if you have ever had someone you love fall prey to something horrible that makes them someone they are not, but if you have, you can attest that you are shaken to your core by it. You doubt your own identity as mother, daughter, sister, or friend to this person. You wonder if you are even worthy to bear that title when it seems you are failing miserably at every turn to provide the help, the care, the patience, and the grace that person needs. The Scriptures don't tell us much about what this mother is experiencing with her daughter, but anyone who has loved someone and watched them suffer knows the desperation with which she approaches Jesus.

And haven't we all been there, feeling like unworthy outsiders crashing the Jesus party, when we have shown up to grovel at his feet, asking for grace for someone we love—just begging him for something, anything, to get us both through? We are so often willing to subscribe ourselves to survival mode when it comes to the Lord, are we not? We wouldn't dare to ask for more than what we deserve, which is really so little when we look at who we are, so we beg for just a bit to get us through. We convince ourselves this is the way to be humble before the Lord: not to be presumptuous with our request for his healing nor assume we merit our miracle, when we know well enough that we have too often been outsiders to God's kingdom.

A truly humble person takes courage in her own unworthiness and grows more rather than less hopeful when she realizes what an outsider she is to Jesus. The humblest of hearts are also some of the most bold, brave hearts when they find themselves before the King. They know they merit nothing of their own accord or status, so there is a sense that there is, therefore, nothing for them to lose. St. Thérèse referred to the courage she received from the unfettered trust she learned to place in God as "a holy daring" that was being born within her (see John Udris's book *Holy Daring: The Fearless Trust of St. Thérèse of Lisieux*).

I think it must have been a similar daring that was born in the heart of our Syrophoenician friend as she drew near to Jesus. She may not have been a child of Israel for whom he had come, she may not have fit the definitions of one he would have chosen to draw near to him, but she needed him and she knew it, and she trusted that he would respond. She believed, not in only in Jesus's *ability* to help her, but in his *desire* to help her.

She approaches Jesus, draws near to him, and something springs up in her, a hope for which she has no explanation, and taking into account her own unworthiness to ask him for anything, she approaches him anyway and asks with great courage for what she needs. Oh, how I want to be a woman with faith like that, with courage like that before my Lord!

I too often convince myself that there is some magic theological formula to getting what we want or need from the Lord. If I behave correctly, become the person I need to be, pray the right prayers, then I will be worthy to ask God for the big stuff, for the miracle-level things I need. Then it will be okay for me really to draw near to Jesus and show him my heart. Until then, I'll take the scraps of his love and make do.

But this woman, she teaches us all a lesson in the holy daring that can be ours in Christ if we will place our trust in him and in his goodness. She approaches him with her need, seemingly prepared for what his likely answer will be. She is not put off, offended, or ashamed when she is reminded of her unworthiness. It is a fact she knew when she drew near to him in the first place. She does not see his mention of it as a rejection of her, but as a simple statement of an obvious fact, a statement that, rather than closing the door on her request, opens the door for further conversation.

I do not know about you, but I am not quite sure how I would react if Jesus turned to me in my desperation and reminded me that I was not in the fold of God's children but merely a dog, a stray unworthy of the grace for which I was begging. Actually, I do know, because I have felt rejected and rebuffed by the Lord before, and I regret to say I have not always responded with the humble trust and gracious perseverance of the Syrophoenician woman.

Like the times I ate the scraps off my kids' plates, feeling grumpy and hungry at the end of a long day, I developed a preprogrammed response when Jesus offered me a little faith challenge. I would try to figure out how to make do on "not enough," so I didn't have to humble myself to beg for more. The role of the unworthy beggar, theoretically speaking, sounds romantic to me, but when I am faced with the reality, I am tempted not to see it as an invitation from Jesus to go deeper in my relationship with him, but as a reason to look for my own way through.

But how much our Gospel friend here has to teach me about who my Jesus really is and who I can be in him! This woman, the one who is not supposed to "get" Jesus, not supposed to understand who he is, gets it perfectly well. She knows that she can be courageous and approach him with boldness because she trusts that he is good. She knows she is unworthy to approach him, but she is not counting on her own worthiness to earn her a miracle—she is counting on the compassion of his heart, flinging herself into the arms of mercy. She begs even for just a scrap of it, as if the nearness of her encounter with him has given her a whiff of his kindness and she is trailing the scent— like a dog on the hunt.

What we see as a stiff, terse response is actually Jesus's offering an opportunity for a heart to be truly revealed for what it is. And our Syrophoenician sister, with her eyes of humble faith, receives his words as an invitation to enter into conversation with the good man that she has come to believe has the power to save her from the enemy's hold on what she values most.

Sometimes when Jesus offers unexpected answers like this in the Gospels, I sort of sit with it uncomfortably, wondering what to make of it. I mean, he doesn't seem like a very nice guy if you take this response at face value. When I come to Jesus with what feels like a desperate circumstance, and he directs me to an unexpected answer like this one, I am tempted to feel as if he is just being mean, or unfair, or maybe doesn't even really love me. It is hard for me, in my own hunger, to remember that, when Jesus refuses the easy answer, it is almost always because he is waiting for an opportunity to show us a bit of his glory. Jesus faithfully uses our desperate circumstances to prove to us that he knows just what we need and how best to provide it to us, even when it seems impossible—and often that provision looks a little like a miracle.

There is a lesson for me in the response of this woman, whose humility breeds both boldness and acceptance in her heart. She does not slink away from Jesus's answer with a rejected countenance. No, she presses in; she perseveres in faith. And in her humility, she is able to remind Jesus of who he is, to prick the well of compassion and mercy that are just waiting to flow forth from his heart to her. She counters his off-putting answer with her own surprising response. It is a wholehearted testimony of her faith in him. If he will not give her his best, she knows that just a bit will be enough. She will make do with the scraps if they are all he will give, because she believes so fully in him, she who is not even supposed to know about the coming Messiah. She believes that even a bit of him is better than none at all.

But our Jesus is not the kind to send us away half-full when we long to be completely filled by him. He is not one to deny our desire and our hunger for him when we approach him in humble faith and wholehearted hope. No, he wants to feed us until we have had our fill of him, until we have drawn so near and have drunk so deeply of him that we are overflowing with the grace and the mercy and the tenderness he has offered us.

We can be bold in asking our Lord for what we need, despite all the things that might disqualify us and make us unworthy— that is, if that boldness comes from a humble heart and a persistent faith that he has all that we need and more: the kind of faith that would lead us to accept scraps from his table with grateful hearts if it is what he desires to offer us.

It is that kind of faith that draws the heart of Jesus to us and makes us irresistible to him. It is the faith of the saints. It is the faith of the Syrophoenician woman. It was the faith too of his Mother, Mary, who we often find boldly approaching him with questions or requests that he finds irresistible. Remember her questions to the young Jesus found in the Temple, which he answers in patient kindness, her request at Cana, which he grants with graciousness. She is irresistible to him because she is the perfection of a humble heart and a persistent faith. And he desires to fill the longings of those kinds of hearts, not just with a bit of his love and mercy, but with all of himself, until they are filled up to overflowing.

Don't we women need to be allowed to sit and take in that message? Don't we need to hear it deep in our bones? Because so many of our days are plagued with the doubt that we deserve anything at all from our Jesus, much less the full measure of his love.

I too am often quick to see Jesus's replies to me as rejections rather than as an opportunity to make myself irresistible to him with my humble faith and wild hope. I think he is telling me, "Oh no, I cannot possibly do that. There is not enough of me to waste on someone like you." And so I nod in agreement and list all the ways he could be right, all the ways I am not worthy of the fullness of his love: "You're right, Lord. There is not enough here for you to consider worthy of a miracle—not enough grace, not enough patience, not enough goodness, not enough holiness. I am not enough, Lord." But in truth what Jesus desires is that I simply take one step closer, draw a little nearer, and profess that I believe he is enough, has enough, loves enough, to make of me what I cannot make of myself.

I think of how often I have prayed for my children, my husband, the moms we minister to, people I love, with a certain sort of trepidation, feeling almost sorry for them that it was me they had to rely on to do the asking for them. I can forget to have courage before the Lord at times because I come to him convinced that the answer to my prayers lies in something I must do rather in the way that I ask.

But I have seen him do some amazing things when I have embraced the courage of our Syrophoenician friend, the courage of one who asks with a humble and grateful heart. When I dare to ask boldly because I believe in who he is more than I believe in what I want from him, the prayer that results is a whisper of hope that pulls Jesus to me and releases the great flood of his love and mercy over me.

~ Who Does He Say You Are? ~

An Invitation to Dare

Every year since Bryce has died, I have asked other mothers to share their prayer intentions with me so that I can carry them through my days during the months that made up his short life. From May until September, I am entrusted with the most noble, loving, caring requests from mothers, most often desperate to see God do something for someone they love. I carry them with an acute awareness of the deep privilege it is to be entrusted with them, and in turn, they remind me of the rich treasure I have in my sweet little saint, who echoes my bold faith before the Lord's throne.

So much hope has been born in my heart in those days and weeks as I have watched miracles happen for other mothers: an unlikely adoption completed in record time, the conversion of a child back to his faith, the healing of hurting hearts, the rapid growth of our life-saving ministry to indigenous mothers, babies who have lived when circumstances predicted otherwise. I always go into those prayers with a daring I often lack in my own personal prayers. I am so certain of his love for the hearts of these mothers, of his love for this little one of mine who now enjoys his eternal company, that I am consumed by an unrelenting hope that draws me past my doubts and insecurities. In those weeks of prayer, I am so aware of how near this Jesus of ours is, and how easily he is drawn to the pleading of our humble hearts. I am ready to answer any challenge he lays before me, because I know he asks out of love and returns only mercy for my feeble attempts at a worthy answer.

Yet, even with that assurance, I can so easily forget to approach Jesus with a humble and expectant, courageous prayer for what I personally need from him to survive. I so easily fall prey to the pride that convinces me that if I can't get it right on my own, I am not even worthy of the scraps from him.

But Jesus just wants to hear me ask. He is just waiting for me to say that I believe he will do what I ask him to do. And then he reaches out and places his hands on me, not to give me his leftover love, but to fill me up to overflowing with it. He is so ready to run to us, if only we will pray with the kind of faith that makes us, not worthy of him, but irresistible to him.

This is the way of our God with us, friends. We assume rejection of our prayers whereas he is inviting us to radical faith. We assume our unworthiness whereas he waits to see a hope that he cannot resist.

"For saying that, you may go," he tells us her. Her prayer has been answered. Her daughter has been healed because of this mother's humble faith and persistent prayer. This woman becomes the living example of the parable he once told about a widow who persisted in her asking until she got what she needed. She shows us how we can make ourselves irresistible to Christ with truly courageous prayer.

Whether our prayers are answered is not dependent upon our worthiness or even the quality of our understanding of who Jesus is. He is not drawn to our theological astuteness or our social status. He is drawn to our hearts. And the more we draw near to him and remember that it is in him that we find our worth, the more we can approach him with a holy daring, a boldness that comes from our hope in him rather than in our confidence in ourselves.

You might start out small, just asking for the scraps of what Jesus has to offer, hoping to get enough to share with the ones you love. But he never asks you to give anything away before he has filled you up to overflowing. He does not send you away half-filled when you approach him with full faith. He longs instead for you to bring him what faith you have in boldness, in confidence that he can respond with a disproportionate grace. Then he desires to bear witness to the miracle of your faith and confidence becoming more than you could have ever imagined they could be. In the sweet excitement of having been met where you are by divine grace and then transformed, you can offer the overflow of that grace freely to the ones you love and have longed for him to heal.

I think of the way he feeds us with his very life, his Body and Blood in the Holy Eucharist. We can never be enough to merit that kind of mercy, yet Jesus comes to us out of love. We know that even the tiniest scrap, or smallest crumb, of one host still holds the fullness of the Body, Blood, soul, and divinity of Jesus. There are no scraps of his Holy Presence. He gives himself fully to us, even in these simple forms. And because the Eucharist is an unearned gift of grace, we can approach with a humble faith and open our mouths to consume our God. There is no greater act of boldness or courage than that, friends! He longs to fill you there, in the Blessed Sacrament, just as he longs to fill you daily with his Word and with the miracle of grace.

So listen to the longings of your heart, friend, and don't be afraid to bring them to Jesus. Approach him as one who knows her own smallness but believes in his greatness. Be bold in asking for what you know you do not deserve but believe he has the power to give freely. Lean into the holy daring that is the courage of a humble heart, and let your faith be tested and found true. Ask and ask again when our Lord invites you. Hope in the very best he has to offer; look for the fullest manifestation of his glory.

And then watch how he is drawn to you, friend. See how you become too lovely for him to resist. Watch him draw near and lay his hands on your problems, your hopes, your needs, and make miracles happen. Receive the fullness of his love and his grace and his tender mercy. And then go. Go back and love the way that he has loved you, with a humble and grateful heart.

~ LET US PRAY ~

Jesus, maker of miracles, filler of souls, I have so often assumed this life you call me to goes in reverse from the way you really intended it. I have too often thought that I am called to make myself worthy of what I ask of you. In my misguided economy, I come up with an anemic faith and a malnourished spirit that asks wrongly.

Help me, Lord, to remember your faithfulness before I consider my own worthiness. Give me a heart that is filled with courage to ask for what I need because it is filled with faith in who you are. Keep near to my thoughts the miracles you make for those who approach with humble hearts and persistent faith.

Help me to train my spirit to accept your invitation to profess my faith in you more fully, to forget myself more completely, rather than to run away licking the wounds of rejection. Give me a hope so bold that I will see every challenge as an invitation, a welcome to woo your heart with my confidence in you.

Lord, I want to be a woman who is irresistible to you, who draws your heart to mine with my relentless pursuit of the love and mercy only you can give. I want to be a woman who has the kind of faith that is willing to accept the scraps because I am so sure that even a bit of you is enough—a woman who walks away from you filled to overflowing because you cannot resist that kind of faith.

Here is my first bold prayer, Lord. I pray it in humble hope and expectant faith. Make me a woman like that, a woman like my Syrophonenician sister. I believe you can, and I believe you will. Amen.

~ QUESTIONS FOR REFLECTION ~

1. Is there anything I need for which I have been afraid to ask Jesus? What makes me scared to approach Jesus?

2. What is my normal response when Jesus does not answer my prayers right away, or when he challenges my faith with an unexpected answer?

3. Would I consider myself bold or daring in my relationship with Christ? Do I feel certain that he loves me and wants to answer my prayers?

4. How might I pray more boldly and more humbly? What is my irresistible prayer?

CHAPTER ELEVEN

"YOUR PRESENCE MATTERS"
Mary, the Wife of Clopas

Meanwhile, standing near the cross of Jesus were his mother, and his mother's sister, Mary the wife of Clopas, and Mary Magdalene. When Jesus saw his mother and the disciple whom he loved standing beside her, he said to his mother, "Woman, here is your son." Then he said to the disciple, "Here is your mother." And from that hour the disciple took her into his own home.

—JOHN 19:25–27

. . . . .

I've never been one to bear my own suffering in a way that anyone would consider particularly saintly. I'm a quitter and a complainer and a slack-kneed coward more than I am righteous and virtuous in God's sight, for sure. But as bad as I am at carrying my own cross, I am way, way worse at help-lessly watching someone I love suffer. I am a fixer by nature, and not being able to fix a circumstance that is causing pain to someone I love makes me frustrated and uncomfortable. Often, it is easier to walk away than to face my own helplessness, to avoid the pain altogether rather than to acknowledge that it is there and there is no way I can stop it.

A well-loved Christian blogger, Kara Tippets, who died last year from brain cancer, wrote a book during her battle and treatment titled *Just Show Up: The Dance of Walking Through Suffering Together.* The title reveals the heart of her message. Walking through her darkest days and hardest battle, the one thing she longed for most, needed most, from her friends and community and people who loved her, was for them just to show up. Even when it was hard, even when they were unsure what to do or say or how to act, even when there was nothing they could do to make it better, she longed for them just to come and be present to her.

We are quick to dismiss the value of our presence, to assume that if we cannot be of physical help to someone, if there is nothing for us to "do," no way for us tangibly to make things better, then there is no reason for us to show up.

Jesus had thousands of followers by the time we arrive at this scene in the Gospels, the moment of his death on the cross. He had an intimate circle of friends whom he had poured life and truth and hope into over the course of his three years in public ministry. They had seen miracles, seen the blind see and the lame walk, watched Lazarus walk out from the tomb, seen the loaves multiplied. They had broken bread with him and seen him pray the agonizing prayers of a million brokenhearted souls. Jesus had offered them full view of both his majestic divinity and his vulnerable humanity. Yet, at the moment of his death, Scripture tells us that of all those friends, only four remained, and three of them were women—his Mother, his Mother's sister, and Mary Magdalene. And with them was his beloved disciple, John.

We know Jesus's Mother, Mary, well by the time we see her here, standing at the foot of his cross. We are certainly not surprised by her presence. She is his Mother and his perfect disciple. She follows him where he goes, even unto a tortuous death on a cross. We know something too of Mary Magdalene, who was a faithful follower and soon becomes the first witness to the resurrection. The third woman, though, who is called Mary, the wife of Clopas, his Mother's sister, is unknown to us; all that we know of her is that she was present at the foot of his cross. And it is enough to know, because that simple act of loyalty, not to look away from such a gruesome scene, but to stay and stand with the others, is gift enough. This Mary's presence matters.

I cannot imagine what it was like to watch Jesus suffer the tortuous death he endured. I do not pretend to understand the environment that surrounded the moments of his passion: the crowds, the tension, the hatred that filled the air. I can only try to guess at the fear, the anguish, and the utter helplessness and despair that his friends and followers felt as he was hoisted up on the cross, already broken, bruised, and bloody, covered in the spittle of being despised and scorned, his head pierced with the thorns of a thousand accusations.

I do not know what it took to be the ones who stayed rather than the ones who fled. But from what we know of those left standing at the foot of the cross, the courage to remain was present in women.

It is Woman, Mary, who first receives the announcement that he is to come into this world, and it is she who receives his lifeless body from the cross. Later, it will be another woman, another Mary who is present here at the cross, who first witnesses his resurrection glory. And there is a third Mary here, a woman about whom we know little else other than that she was present at the cross. Women are a near constant presence in the Gospels, always showing up where Jesus shows up, always appearing when he steps on the scene. Perhaps Mary, the wife of Clopas, had learned that kind of loyalty from watching Jesus's

Mother, a close family member, all the years she stood by his side, a model of fidelity. Maybe this was one of many moments she had accompanied his Mother at his side. What we know for certain is this: this woman, this Mary, draws near to him and stays through the darkest moments of salvation history.

And I think that says something about us as women, we who bear him as light and stand with him in the darkest hour. We are wired to draw near to our God, wired to seek him and serve him and sit with him, wired for connection and closeness and vulnerable friendship with the heart of our Savior. We are made to know and love him so that we can be transformed by that love. And yet, how difficult it is to be the one who stands and watches him suffer with nothing more to offer than your presence! Is it enough just to let your heart break with your brokenhearted God?

How many things in our world today ask the very same of us? Daily we are bombarded with images and stories of a world suffering and broken. We wonder how to be Christ, how to be love, to so much pain and loss. We stand in the tension between wanting to be able to do something, anything, to fix the brokenness of the world in which we live and needing to be present right here in our homes, in our lives, at the kitchen sink and the bed side and the carpool line and the office. We can't fix it, and there are more hurting places than we could ever reach. So what do we have to offer in the face of such sadness, such darkness?

Presence, friends. This presence is the merciful love of one, like this Mary, wife of Clopas, who stands at the foot of the cross, the humble wisdom of knowing that your presence matters. Suffering and pain and loss loom all around us, and most of it is not ours to remedy, much of it will not be undone until this kingdom is eclipsed by the heavenly one. Our only option is to choose to be present to the suffering, to stand and stay and not run from it. It hardly seems a gift most of the time, but it is treasured by our Jesus, our Savior, who looks down from his own cross and sees us. He sees us standing there, embracing the suffering alongside him, and he is moved by it.

Running from suffering seems to be as much a part of our human nature as being drawn to the heart of the Savior is part of our spiritual instinct. It can pose an interesting dichotomy when the Savior to whom we are drawn is one who suffers, and whose suffering is the result of our own faults and failings. How do we find the strength to stay through the labored breathing and death rattle of our God when it is we who have condemned him? I cannot pretend to know, really, but perhaps the answer is love.

When the moment comes to face the most unbearable suffering imaginable, we find the courage to stand our ground by knowing that our presence is enough to please our God, that it is a balm to the heart of our Savior. We find our strength in knowing that, when our God took human form and then took on the suffering of all humanity, the presence of three women at the foot of the cross was enough to make him turn his head and take notice. We embrace wholeheartedly the upside-down reality that showing up and being present isn't the thing we do because we can't do anything more; it's the thing we do because it is what he most desires of us, and it is the greatest gift we have to offer. Drawing near to the suffering one who has drawn near to us is the ultimate act of friendship with Christ. We find the courage to love him in his suffering in the way that he has loved us in our sin.

In our ministry to indigenous mothers, I encounter suffering on a daily basis that I long to be able to fix. I hunger for justice for these women whom I have come to love—women who face harsh burdens of poverty, of being voiceless, many of whom face abuse, neglect, and lack of access to education and health care. They suffer so many wrongs that I long to right. I have to fight the urge nearly constantly to ask them all to stay forever, just to live with us indefinitely while I try to fix all the things that make their lives hard and bring them pain. I lament to my husband regularly, and he just as often reminds me that if we made it our business to solve all the problems and bear all the burdens of even one of these women, we would be undone, over with, in short order. We do not have the resources to fix the brokenness that brings them to us. What we have and what God has called us to offer these women is a willingness to sit with them in their time of crisis, a willingness to enter into their pain as they labor and give birth far from home in a place that feels scary and strange, and often in circumstances that are less than joyous, a willingness to sit beside them as they hold a sick and feverish child in their arms and wait out the worst of it. This is what I can give them: my presence and the comfort of a warm plate of food, a friendly face, safety, and rest. I cannot take away the suffering, but I can show up, enter in, and be present.

This was enough for Mary to offer Jesus as she stood at the foot of the cross, and it is enough for me to offer now. What about you, friend? Do you feel tempted to run from the face of suffering because you are undone by your inability to do anything to fix it? Do you doubt you are worth anything to those who are suffering around you, to this wide and broken world we call home?

Can you dare to believe that your good and faithful God only desires that you recognize him in the suffering, draw near, and stand with him? Can you dare to hope that your presence matters that much to him? Yes, friend, you can. Because here, in the darkest moment of his earthly life, his comfort is in the presence of his Mother and his friends. He turns his face to them, notices them, and then calls them into a ministry of presence to one another. "Woman, here is your son," he says to his Mother. And to the disciple he says, "Here is your mother." And the Scriptures say that from then on he "took her into his own home."

Jesus's suffering is nearing its end, climaxing here in this scene, but the suffering of the world he leaves behind is only beginning. And one of his last commands to the woman he called "Mother" and the disciple he called "friend" at the foot of the cross was, not to stop what they had begun there in that moment, but to continue to draw near to one another in their pain and loss as they had drawn near to him in his. Their presence mattered to him, and since our hearts reflect his own, presence matters to us too. Our being present to the suffering that we face ourselves, and our standing beside our neighbor who suffers—both of these matter to our God; we are able to offer ourselves as consolation to him, and he is moved by our offering.

~ Who Does He Say You Are? ~

An Invitation to Witness

Recently, my husband and I were invited to Rome to share the story of our mission with Cardinal Fernando Filoni, the prefect for the Vatican's Congregation for the Evangelization of Peoples. This is the organization that oversees all missionary activity in the Catholic Church. Cardinal Filoni is a prominent leader, and I felt overwhelmed as I waited to meet him. What should my husband and I tell him? What would he even want to know about us? What could I say about our work with a tiny group of people in a remote corner of the world, such a very long way from Rome? I mean, I love sharing my little saint's story and the joy of our missionary calling with people I encounter, but it hardly seems worthy to interrupt the busy schedule of the man who is overseeing the missionary activity of the entire Church.

What I did not expect was that Cardinal Filoni would come to us with the tender heart of a shepherd, already knowing our story, to offer affirmation and joy and a fatherly blessing! But the moment that most took my breath away came when the cardinal turned to me, looked me straight in the eyes, and said these words to me regarding my son's death: "When you were sitting there in your pain and suffering, God stopped and he saw you. He looked at you. And in that moment, he chose you."

I am stunned. And it would have been hard for me to believe his words, to grasp them fully, if I had not come to know Jesus in the way I have since the days he tucked me away in a hidden corner of the world, sat me on a riverbank, and reminded me of who I was through the stories that show us who he is. I could have faith in the cardinal's kind words, believe in the tender mercy they imparted, because I know this story. And I know that my life is only repeating the story of my sisters who also once stood facing the most unbearable suffering and pain, when God turned and saw them, when he called them.

Yes, sister, our presence matters because suffering is the economy of salvation, and we cannot escape it if we wish to enter into intimacy with the Savior who bore our sins unto death on a cross. Our presence matters, because in the face of that reality, what he longs for most is the assurance that he is loved in return for so great a sacrifice. Our presence matters because our willingness to stand and face the pain of our own suffering turns his face to us and calls us into friendship with him and communion with one another. We are transformed by our own commitment to being present because it draws Jesus's gaze to us. When we are willing to offer love when love is all we have to offer, he is moved to see us and call us into service to him and one another.

Just show up. This is the lesson of Mary, Jesus's Mother, throughout most of Jesus's public life. Over and over again in the Gospels, once Jesus is an adult and has entered his ministry, all that is mentioned of Mary is that she was present. This too is the lesson of Mary her sister, the wife of Clopas, at the foot of the cross. And it is the lesson we, dear sister, are called to offer our hurting world.

We cannot fix all the hurt and pain in this world, we cannot even fix most of the hurt and pain in our own lives. We are not called to. There is only one Savior who can bear that pain on his shoulders and redeem it, and he has already done that, once and for all. So while we wait for his coming glory, while we walk the road between here and heaven, what we have to offer is presence—the consolation that we do not turn and run, that we show up and we stay and we love the hurting hearts in our midst and accept the reality of suffering. Presence is the gift we bring to the heart of this suffering world and to our Lord. And it is the gift he most desires. It is a gift that matters.

Let us then, sister, take our place beside the women of the cross. Let us be present to the God who bears our pain and redeems our loss with his very life. And let us be assured that it is enough to turn his heart to us and ours to him. Let us live present to the importance of our presence.

~ LET US PRAY ~

O my Jesus, Crucified One, I look around at the world in which I live, and I see so much pain, so much loss. It all echoes your suffering face on the cross. I long to have something to offer that will make it better, make it go away. Yes, sometimes I am even tempted to turn my back and run, Lord, because I cannot bear to see so many hurting hearts and to feel so helpless.

But, you, my sweet Savior, do not call me to take on the burdens of that pain and loss; that is your job, and you have done it once and for all. You allow me to see that pain so that I can choose to love, choose to stand, choose to stay in the face it. You offer me the chance to show up, love, and know that it matters to you.

Lord, let me embrace that opportunity. Let me see suffering in my own life and in the world around me as an opportunity to be present to you, my brokenhearted Savior, an opportunity to allow my heart to be pierced by the pain and not to look away. Let me see it as an opportunity to assure your sacrifice of love has moved me to love.

Teach me to be the woman who shows up and stays, Lord, even when the pain seems unbearable—who stays long enough to see you stop and turn your face to me, long enough to hear your call to do the same for my brothers and sisters here on earth.

Lord, I long to be like the women at the foot of your cross who knew their presence mattered. Give me the grace to stand with you long enough, to love you deeply enough, to draw near enough to your suffering heart that I know that to love is to show up and embrace the truth that presence is the most desired gift of all. Amen.

~ Questions for Reflection ~

1. When has someone made a difference in my suffering, simply by showing up?
2. When have I had an opportunity to be present to someone in his or her suffering?

3. Who is one person in my life who needs me to show up and to offer support in his or her time of pain or suffering?
4. Where am I experiencing suffering in my life? Have I drawn near to the suffering heart of the Savior to tell him about it?

CHAPTER TWELVE

"You Were Made for Resurrection Joy"

Mary Magdalene

Early on the first day of the week, while it was still dark, Mary Magdalene came to the tomb and saw that the stone had been removed from the tomb. So she ran and went to Simon Peter and the other disciple, the one whom Jesus loved, and said to them, "They have taken the Lord out of the tomb, and we do not know where they have laid him." Then Peter and the other disciple set out and went toward the tomb. The two were running together, but the other disciple outran Peter and reached the tomb first. He bent down to look in and saw the linen wrappings lying there, but he did not go in. Then Simon Peter came, following him, and went into the tomb. He saw the linen wrappings lying there, and the cloth that had been on Jesus' head, not lying with the linen wrappings but rolled up in a place by itself. Then the other disciple, who reached the tomb first, also went in, and he saw and believed; for as yet they did not understand the scripture, that he must rise from the dead. Then the disciples returned to their homes.

But Mary stood weeping outside the tomb. As she wept, she bent over to look into the tomb; and she saw two angels in white, sitting where the body of Jesus had been lying, one at the head and the other at the feet. They said to her, "Woman, why are you weeping?" She said to them, "They have taken away my Lord, and I do not know where they have laid him." When she had said this, she turned around and saw Jesus standing there, but she did not know that it was Jesus. Jesus said to her, "Woman, why are you weeping? Whom are you looking for?" Supposing him to be the gardener, she said to him, "Sir, if you have carried him away, tell me where you have laid him, and I will take him away." Jesus said to her, "Mary!" She turned and said to him in Hebrew, "Rabbouni!" (which means Teacher). Jesus said to her, "Do not hold on to me, because I have not yet ascended to the Father. But go to my brothers and say to them, 'I am ascending to my Father and your Father, to my God and your God.'" Mary Magdalene went and announced to the disciples, "I have seen the Lord"; and she told them that he had said these things to her.

—JOHN 20:1–18

• • • • •

Mary Magdalene has come prepared to mourn. She had been one of the ones who had the courage to stay with Jesus until the very end, one of the three women still at the foot of the cross when Jesus breathed his last. And this morning, she comes to weep. It's as if all the courage she mustered at the foot of the cross now comes leaking out in the sorrow of having lost one she loved, one who showed her a new way, one she followed and cared for and was transformed by.

Her sadness has finally overcome her, and she comes to his tomb to weep. She is compelled to the tomb alone while the darkness of night still hangs on the air. And there she weeps.

Night's darkness seems terribly long to a restless, grieving soul. The silence weighs heavy, and haunting memories loom large in the space between dreams and reality. During the first nights after experiencing the death of a loved one, the mourners are often restless, unable to sleep well. I remember telling a friend the day after we buried Bryce that I would be okay if night never came. I would prowl the floors in the predawn hours feeling a panic rising in my chest. I just needed the sun to rise, needed desperately to cling to the hope of tomorrow, needed release from the deafening silence of loss and the creeping desperation of dark sorrow.

I imagine that desperation might have been what drove Mary Magdalene to Jesus's tomb in the darkness. She was desperate to find a way to wait for the light to dawn, desperate to escape the darkness of her broken heart. She wanted to weep alone, away from the crowds, where she could break open and set free the sorrow that was eating her from the inside out. And she hoped with every fiber of her sad spirit that soon the sun would rise.

Oh, little did she know! Does it not make your skin tingle, the knowing with which we can watch Mary Magdalene come to the tomb? Our awareness of what awaits her might make us underestimate the humanity that accompanied Mary in that dark moment, the ache that preceded her to the tomb. But we would do well to remember it because we have felt it too, have we not? Each of us carries different burdens of sorrow, but we all carry them. What breaks our hearts might be different, but we all have known the moment when our broken hearts compel us away to weep alone, waiting desperately for hope to come to us in the darkness. We all know the grief that brought Mary Magdalene to the tomb that morning, and the hint of hope that kept her looking back to her Jesus for an answer: What do I do now, Lord? How do I keep going?

Mary Magdalene was not a casual mourner. No, she came with all the sorrow of mourning a loved one whom she had watched endure horrible suffering, whose body she had helped to anoint and wrap and lay lifeless in a hewn-out hole. She came to weep for Jesus of Nazareth, the one whom she had grown to love with the affection with which one loves a friend and a man whom she had come to believe was God. It was a personal grief, an intimate sorrow, that brought Mary Magdalene to tears at the tomb, that compelled her to draw near to her Jesus one more time. And it was that intimate drawing near that positioned her to be the first witness to his rising.

And for us too, this is the key to resurrection hope. We can truly know the relief of his rising when we move past a casual admiration of our Savior and toward a relationship based on the true conversion of our hearts, a metanoia that makes us no longer interested outsiders but members of the family of Christ, sisters who mourn that he had to be lost to death in order for us to be saved.

One day not long ago, in an unassuming church on a side street of Rome, my husband and I walked into the most unexpected of sights. We wandered in the dimly lit grandness of an old church, taking in the details of art and architecture that turn the mind and heart in silence toward all things sacred and holy. We separated, I drawn to one thing and he to another, until my eye caught him approaching me with an urgent hurry in his step, waving me to come. He grabbed me by the hand and led me to a small rectangular window in a little nook of the church, where my eyes stopped to read the sign that marked it: "The foot of Mary Magdalene." Inside was a small reliquary in the perfect form of a foot that held, purportedly, the bones of the foot of Mary Magdalene. But the relics themselves were really beside the point in that moment, because my heart was already caught up in the simple yet profound truth of the importance of that foot, her foot: it was the first foot to enter the tomb of the risen Christ.

My heart thumps fast again every time I think of it, standing there in this shadowy corner face-to-face with the reality that the first foot to make its way into the resurrected life was real, not the thing of tall tales and legends. It was a real human foot made of the same bones and sinews and tissues that mine is, and it was the foot of a woman! It was the foot of one who had drawn near to Christ in both life and death, who grieved him with a quiet intimacy, and then saw the hope of our salvation, our Jesus in his risen form, before any other human did.

Now, I am well aware that the resurrection is for all of us, man and woman alike. But there is something that speaks so deeply to my feminine heart about this encounter. A woman's heart is programmed for connection. We are rarely casual disciples of anything. I mean, I can easily become passionate about a thousand things on any given day and feel an attachment to them—from the women who walk through my door to have their needs met, to the guy singing that one song alone in the church on YouTube, to that family who needs help covering medical costs. My heart feels things on a personal level in a way that I know is uniquely linked to my feminine makeup.

Peter and John, it seems, engage the idea of Jesus's going missing from the tomb with curiosity. They enter, look around, see he is not there, and come to believe that he must be risen, and then they turn to head toward home.

And then there is Mary Magdalene, who doesn't follow them home. She leans into the tomb looking for evidence of where he might be, of what might have happened, leading with her weeping, feeling heart.

"Why are you weeping?" the angels ask her as she leans into the tomb. Mary Magdalene is not ashamed of her emotion; she is not hesitant in her answer. She is missing her Lord. No, she does not fully grasp the great theological mysteries of the passion and the resurrection that she is about to encounter. She cannot explain that she leans in to look because everything about Jesus indicated there was something greater coming on the other side of his hideous death. All she knows is that she is there because she is looking for her Lord. And that is enough to lead her straight to the Resurrected One.

What a joyful affirmation for my feeling, feminine heart!

Mary Magdalene turns from the tomb to the face of Christ; she is the first to experience the metanoia of redemption. And with her, all of us can experience the same, by turning our broken hearts and our sin-stained souls and the world's economy of justice upside down with our wildly loving, deeply feeling hearts. O, sister, turn with me, turn to him, and offer him that heart of yours, with all its weeping and wondering and hopeful desperation; and know it deep inside your soul—you too were made for resurrection joy.

"Mary!" he calls, as you might call to a friend who doesn't yet recognize you, and in the sound of his voice, she is fully convinced, her heart's conversion is complete, and she has made her full metanoia. She is Mary of the resurrection, the one to behold first the human form of our salvation. "Rabbouni," she calls back in Hebrew, "Teacher." In the speaking of their two names, there is an unspoken lesson. Her joy abounds because she knows this Jesus well, she recognizes his voice and the way he says her name, and she responds to him affectionately, calling him back by the name she has called him so many times. Mary's joy is the joy of one who has a friendship restored, a loved one thought lost returned; she is one who expected to weep forever finding out that she can instead rejoice.

One recent afternoon, I stood at the bottom of the jungle hill that is now my front yard. My five sons and my husband and I were wet and soapy, and laughter shook us from head to toe. Our house mom, Susana, who works with us every day in our ministry, stood at the window laughing too. And mamas from a faraway mountain land that I could never have even dreamed of a few short years ago cuddled their babies in rocking chairs on my patio and laughed their stunned heads off at us. My boys and their dad had built an industrial-level waterslide out of some huge old tarps, a hose, a packet of laundry detergent, and the slope of our hill. The joy of that slide was irresistible to even my more cautious mother heart. I threw on some shorts and joined them in the sliding.

As I stood there at the bottom of that hill watching the fullness of my life come hurling toward me in the soapy figures of my little boys and the wild laughter of women I have come to love, I laughed deep and strong, with my whole body. And I was fully aware that it was not simply the laughter of having fun. It was a true and lasting joy that invaded my body and that shook it with giggles. It was the joy of one who has known loss and found redemption, of one who has seen a tiny glimpse of the other side of the story.

If you had tried to tell me back in the days of the riverbank that this is what my life would be like now, that I would know such deep and unshakeable joy, it would have been nearly impossible for me to believe. I needed the quiet days of drawing near to the tomb and looking for my Jesus in order to know the joy I have today.

It was at the riverbank, where I first scratched out the words that have blossomed into this book, that I remembered what his voice sounded like when he called my name. It was in those days that I stopped looking for Jesus in confused sorrow and remembered that he was right here, already having defeated death and made it into victory. At the river, I turned and recognized him once again. And in doing so, I began the slow transformation of myself back into who Jesus made me to be. I know now that it was the resurrected Christ that I encountered below the banana trees. And I know that in that encounter, in that drawing near, he began to remind me of who I truly am—a woman who has suffered, yes, but a woman made to know true joy, a woman called to live a life of rejoicing despite all of the hurts life has meted out, because I am a witness to redemption.

~ Who Does He Say You Are? ~
An Invitation to Resurrected Joy

They say that Mary Magdalene becomes the apostle to the apostles after she encounters Jesus risen. I wonder now if what she might have to teach them is this: the message of a heart that is rejoicing with resurrection joy. Though she is unable to explain what happened or how Christ is here, she explodes with the impetuous and overwhelming joy that it is to recognize the resurrected Christ when he calls your name. I wonder if she was sent out as the apostle of the heart, the one who hurries to where the others, who try to figure it all out with their heads, have gone so she can awaken their hearts. Mary runs out to the apostles to tell them the good news so that they can stop trying to figure out the tomb and simply rejoice.

When she reaches out for Jesus in the garden, he tells her that she cannot hold on to him. As much as I am sure her heart would have liked to stay there in that moment forever, in that cocoon where it was just her and her Lord, her heart awakening to the "alleluia" life of the resurrection, she has a job to do. This joy is not meant only for her. It belongs to all his followers, to the whole world. She is sent to the apostles, who are then sent to the ends of the earth. Mary Magdalene bears the Good News to the Good News bearers. She is the first to know resurrection joy and the first to share it.

Perhaps she did not fully understand what Jesus meant about ascending to his Father or why she could not yet embrace him. But she understood his command to go, and she obeyed it. This is the gift of a heart that leads us to Jesus. We can feel the joy of his presence and recognize the sound of his voice, and whether or not we delve into the deepest theological mysteries, we know how to obey him. This is the call of an apostle of the heart. It was the call of Mary Magdalene, and it is our call, friends.

When he draws near and reveals to you his goodness, when he shows you the path to salvation, when he offers you resurrection joy, you take hold of it with all your heart. And when he sends you out to proclaim it, whether it be to mighty princes or to poor paupers or your next-door neighbors, you obey. You proclaim just what he has asked you to proclaim, and you do it with great joy, because you know well what you have seen and heard. You know this Jesus, your "Rabbouni," and there is no doubt that you "have seen the Lord."

Jesus transforms Mary Magdalene into a rejoicer when she has come to weep, a believer when she feels lost, and a proclaimer when she desires to hold on and stay. The resurrection joy he brings is not a simple happiness at his return; it is a total transformation of Mary as a follower of Christ. This joy brings us out of ourselves and who we thought we would be and into the full life of obedience and hope Jesus has always had waiting for us. This is the life of one who has drawn near to the heart of her Savior and found friendship with him, who has listened closely and learned to recognize when he is calling her name, who has learned to obey even when she doesn't understand, and who goes out to do his will and proclaim his presence when she is sent.

This too is our life, sisters. This is the full circle of our intimate leaning in to Jesus. He draws near to us where he finds us and shows us who we are when we are reflected in his love. We long to experience more of that love, so we draw near to him, always leaning further, looking harder, longing for more. Our Jesus responds by inviting us into a deeply personal friendship with him, in which we enter into his sufferings and also come to know the joy of his resurrection. This is the life of one redeemed by a Savior she has called friend.

Each step we take into deeper, more intimate friendship with Jesus leads us to a fuller knowledge of the joy that is ours in him. And each increase in joy overflows into a command to go out and proclaim the Good News. The world was changed because one woman did just that. Imagine what might happen if all of us followed in the footsteps of Mary Magdalene, charging out into the world as apostles of resurrection joy, proclaiming that we have seen the Lord. Oh, how I long to be part of that metanoia, friend.

My "metanoia moment" came in a literal sending out, a call to share the Good News of Jesus and his resurrection with a people who do not yet know him. Your call to be an apostle of the resurrection may look very different from mine. But whatever it is that Jesus asks you to do after he shows you his resurrected face and calls you by name, you can do it with great joy, sister. You can run after it with your whole heart and lean into the fullness of that joy. Because your Jesus has come to show you that he is alive, that death and loss are defeated, and that he knows just who you are.

Whatever has brought you to the tomb weeping, know that you are made for resurrection joy. Stay, lean in, and look for the Lord. Before you know it, he will be there beside you in all his glory. And he will fill you with a joy that bubbles over and overflows and sends you out as an apostle of the Good News.

And when you see him? Oh, when he calls your name and you recognize his voice? You will be transformed! You, friend, will become a new creation, one who has drawn near to Christ in sickness and in suffering, in sin and shame, and been made new. You will become one who now knows that the end of the story is that he defeats it all and comes back to offer us a life of hope. And then he sends us to offer that hope to a world so desperately in need of it. He is calling your name. Do you recognize his voice? Turn, friend, and in his face, be reminded of who it is he says that you are.

~ LET US PRAY ~

O "Rabbouni," my risen Lord, you are the transformer of hearts. You show us the way out of the tomb into the resurrection life, Lord. You fill us with a joy that cannot be shaken, that fills us and overflows out in the world. I want that joy, Lord.

Give me the grace to lean in and look for you, to draw nearer and nearer to your heart until I know you in a deep and personal way. Help me to be a follower so faithful that the moment you call my name, I recognize your voice and respond.

Lord, make me an apostle of joy. Give me a heart so full of good news that I cannot help but run out to proclaim it. Make me so certain of who you are and who I am in you that I can confidently proclaim to all I meet: "I have seen the Lord."

I want to be your faithful follower, Jesus. Guide my heart into friendship with you, and give me the grace to stay and wait for the redeeming joy you bring. And then let me not be tempted to keep it for myself, but send me out, confident and strong, to bring the Good News to the waiting world.

Amen.

~ QUESTIONS FOR REFLECTION ~

1. Do I have a personal friendship with Jesus? In what ways could I deepen my intimacy with him?
2. What is different about my life because I know Jesus has risen? What does it mean to me to experience the joy of the resurrection?
3. To whom am I being called to proclaim the Good News? Can I do so confidently?
4. How does drawing near to Jesus help me know better who I am?

· · · · ·

Well, friend, here we are. We have come to the end of our journey through the Gospels with the women who knew Jesus personally, who encountered God in human form. We have looked at the women who are examples and friends, who reveal the way in which our Lord loves us and shows us who we are in him. We have looked closely at Mary, the one woman who shows us the full realization of all the possibilities our womanhood holds.

You have come to know too a bit of my personal story, of the way my life has been shaped by both deep sorrow and great joy. I hope I have shown you a full and revealing picture of how Jesus remade me when I was no longer certain who I was anymore—how God loved me with the most tender of mercies through my grief and gave me new life in the most surprising of ways. I hope you have seen the ways he has worked to redeem my story and bring me to the place where I can hold both the pain of loss and the joy of hope in the balance of his love.

I pray that in all the women's stories represented in this book, both the stories of the women of the Gospels and my own story, there is a thread that resonates with your experience. I hope that you have found new insight into your own journey of transformation in Christ on these pages, and that you will take what you have reflected on forward with you as you continue to form and grow your relationship with him.

It is my sincerest hope that, whatever brought you to the pages of this book, you will walk away knowing something more about who you are in the eyes of your heavenly Father than you did before you began. I hope that you have a new curiosity about Scripture and what you can learn from the encounters with God that inhabit its pages. I hope that you see life in those words in a way you hadn't before and find freedom to apply your creative imagination to those stories and turn them over and around until they bring you deeper into the heart of your Savior.

And more than anything, I hope you are encouraged to see the Gospels as an invitation to consider who we are in light of who Christ is and to accept the grace he offers us to be transformed by our encounters with him. I pray that you offer your wholehearted yes to that invitation and begin to explore further and more deeply what the Lord might want to offer you in the study of his Word, the grace of the sacraments, and the wisdom of the Church.

I remember the first Bible I ever really felt was my own, the one that I first fell in love with and began to study with a hungry heart. It was gifted to the participants of my confirmation retreat, a simple paperback version, handed uniformly to each person in the room. But for me, a unique aspect of my relationship with God the Holy Spirit was revealed when that Bible was placed in my hands. I dove into it like a banquet set before a starving woman, tasting every little aspect of it with satisfied appreciation. I highlighted and marked pages with holy cards. I taped the binding together with duct tape when it began to fall apart. That Bible was famous among my friends for its fraying edges and furled pages, for the bookmarks and cards that stuck out willy-nilly from between its pages, and for all the highlighting that made it nearly glow in the dark. I remember how it earned me the moniker "Human Concordance," and friends would come to me when they needed a Scripture quotation for such and such a topic, and I would tell them where to find it.

Being a Bible-study girl in a Catholic world sometimes made me feel a bit out of step with other believers, and yet this habit of studying Scripture has enhanced my relationship with God and given me hope on so many occasions in my life when hope was in short supply. It has been a tool that has walked me through so many stages of my life, from the struggles of a young faith facing the world for the first time, through the hardest days of my motherhood and marriage, and around again to the full circle of my story's redemption.

I have owned many Bibles since that first one, and they have all seen a similar fate. I consume them with a hunger that leaves them worn and battered. But they have been the heart of my personal friendship with Christ over the years. Fed by the sacraments, I felt their grace stirred in my heart by his Word. Embraced by the life of the Church, I have made my Catholic faith personal by getting to know the God of Holy Scripture. Commited to a life of serving him, I have found the Holy Spirit's guidance in the pages of my Bible over and over again.

My identity has been affirmed, refined, and remade by the stories of Jesus in the Scriptures. And because of that, my heart longs for every woman to feel free to seek Jesus confidently in his Word, to apply her creative imagination to the stories and narratives of the Bible, and to find truths about who he is and who he says that we are in those pages. I hope that your journey to draw nearer to the heart of Jesus was enhanced by what you discovered in these pages, but I also hope that it is only the beginning of a long and fruitful search for deeper intimacy with him.

Women have been some of the most cherished friends, faithful followers, and powerful witnesses of Jesus from the very beginning. We, friend, are no different. We have a long line of sisters who lead the way, and we have him, our precious Savior, to remind us who we are. In that knowledge and confidence, we are transformed and sent out to transform our world. And we go out together, a great sisterhood of women who know who they are. I believe that what Jesus showed us—when he crossed so many cultural boundaries in order to draw near and welcome women into friendship with him—is the way he desires for us as women to live and follow him down through the ages, in a deeply personal and intimate drawing near to him.

I pray that in these pages you have felt that drawing, that you have encountered Jesus in new ways and seen yourself in a new light. And I pray that, in his reflection, you know with all certainty who it is he says that you are, and that you will take the joy that is yours in him and become an apostle of Good News to all you meet. You are a friend of God, a dwelling place for his glory, with a voice to proclaim his praise. You can ask boldly of the Savior because, in him, you are redeemed, restored, and bear no shame. You can be content in him, filled to over-flowing, standing tall. You are a witness whose life honors him, your presence matters to him, and you were made to know and share the joy of being the friend of the risen Lord. This is who he says that you are. It is the prayer of my heart that these pages have helped you embrace that truth in a deeper way and that you leave this book feeling more confident in Christ than you have ever felt before.

Thank you for journeying deeper with me into the heart of our Savior. May you continue to discover yourself in the leaning and drawing near, deeper and deeper still, to the God who made you—continuing to learn to embrace who it is he says that you are. And may his Word ever guide you to know more of who you are in him.

ACKNOWLEDGMENTS

· · · · ·

My gratitude goes out to the following people, without whom this book would never have made its way into the world:

My husband, Greg—you are the dreamer of God-sized dreams and the adventurer who pushes me to be more than I could ever be without you. Thank you for seeing me through the eyes of the Father and calling me to more.

My boys—Quinn, Gabriel, Brendan, Evan, and Kolbe—you inspire me to live fully, love well, and laugh often every day. Thank you for making me a mother and showing me what love really means.

My sweet little saint, Bryce—you are never far from me, little one. Thank you for your constant prayers and for keeping my eyes ever trained on eternal things.

My mom, Jeanette—you believed in me before I even knew enough of who I was to believe in myself. Thank you for being my constant cheerleader in life.

My sisters—Shannon, Kieran, Gina, Jackie, and Monique—I have never once felt alone in my life because I knew I had you at my side. Thank you for being constant lights that beckon me back to the place I call home.

To the other sisters in my life—the women who have loved and supported me and my dreams across the years and the miles and the phases—thank you for making my life so rich with grace and lavish with love. You are, every one of you, treasures.

To Susana: You are the secret ingredient to my success. Without you, these words would never have found their way to these pages. Thank you for your tireless gift of care and love for us and our ministry. *Que Dios te page lo que yo no puedo. ¡Y que saves como te amo por siempre!*

To Costa Rica—your mountains and your rivers and your *pura vida* have remade me. Thank you for being the land of my freedom and my wholeness. *Te quiero con todo mi corazon.*

To my editor, Heidi Saxton—you believed in this book from the beginning, and the Spirit made a way for us, together. Thank you for seeing what I saw in these stories and for helping me see some things I had not yet seen, for helping me hone my vision and my craft.

To everyone at Franciscan Media and Servant—taking a chance on a first-time author is no small thing, and it is not lost on me. Thank you for giving me this opportunity.